Great Racing Gambles & Frauds

3

Great Racing Gambles & Frauds

3

Selected and Introduced
by
Richard Onslow

MARLBOROUGH/PUNCHESTOWN

MARLBOROUGH BOOKS
Unit 22, Cheney Manor, Swindon, SN2 2PJ

Punchestown Books
4 Arran Quay, Dublin 7
c/o Mitty's of Queen Street,
9 Queen Street, Melbourne 3000, Victoria, Australia

First published 1993
© Text - R. Onslow & others

Editor: Sir Rupert Mackeson, Bart. (as Rupert Collens)
Typesetting and Origination: Capital City, Swindon

Acknowledgements
The Editor wishes to thank all authors and journalists who have
written especially for this book.

The Editor also wishes to acknowledge, with thanks, permission
from living authors and literary executors to reproduce copyright
material.

Punchestown ISBN 1-873920-12 1
Marlborough ISBN 1-873919- 18 2

Printed in Great Britain by BPCC Wheatons Ltd, Exeter

CONTENTS

THE VALUE OF MONEY

Editor's Note

Where possible in these books I have inserted after the actual figures concerned, a possible modern day equivalent following the lead set by my friend, Paul Mathieu, in his brilliant book *"The Druids Lodge Confederacy"* from which Dickie Onslow reproduced in *Volume one* the whole chapter on Hackler's Pride. The Retail Price Index was only started in 1914. Since 1914 the Government, via its Central Statistical Office, has produced an index of retail prices which makes comparisons readily available. I must express my deep gratitude to the Press Officer and his colleagues at the Central Statistical Office for their help in compiling these books. They have spent many hours on the telephone explaining their weird and wonderful figures.

However, prior to 1914, there are many different expert opinions on the value of money as Paul Mathieu said to me in a letter:

"Divide 433.95 [sic] by the Index number and - Hey Presto! - you have an equivalent for the £1 of today.
This of course fails to take into the account the fact that today's RPI is based on the price changes of commodities - baked beans, detergents, mortgages, video recorders - that were hardly in plentiful supply in 1791, or indeed 1891. But it's the only measurement available."

I have discussed the value of the pound from the 1790s to 1900 with various experts at Universities and the Librarians of such

This series will consist of four volumes; the last of which will be published in the autumn of 1994.

distinguished journals as *The Financial Times* and *The Economist*. Some maintain that there was little falling of the value of money in the 19th Century while others argue it was fairly dramatic. I personally believe that there was a substantial decrease in the purchasing power of money in the first 110 years covered by this book and I have used the figures set out below in my computations.

The figures prior to 1900 are highly questionable and different academics will produce radically different figures but I hope they will give the reader some idea of the sums involved.

"1991/1994 Value of Pound in"

1780 - 1799	-	£375
1800 - 1819	-	£350
1820 - 1839	-	£230
1840 - 1859	-	£170
1860 - 1879	-	£120
1880- 1899	-	£80
1900- 1919	-	£44
1920 - 1939	-	£32
1940's	-	£17
1950's	-	£13
1960's	-	£8

One academic suggested that the value of today's pound in 1820 would have been £2,000 and due to deflation £3,500 in 1840 and £4,000 in 1850. So the figures above are very much *E & OE*.

A curate in one of Charles Dickens' books in 1840 says "I have made my fortune, I have secured a living of £35 a year". What is a living for a Man of the Cloth? Certainly he wasn't going to be paid the equivalent of £125,000 a year which a multiplier of 3,500 would indicate, but he would have been paid more than £6,000 which my multiplier of 170 would indicate .

I am afraid it is nearly an insoluble conundrum.

R.C.

THE ART OF THE TART

('Old Q' Rides a Winner)

Introduction by R.O.: Long before he reached an advanced age, in which he made no attempts be venerable, or even respectable, the fourth Duke of Queensberry was universally known as Old Q.

There were only two places in the world that the Duke loved. One was Newmarket, and the other was Piccadilly. On the Heath he could gamble to his heart's content, winning huge sums from his fellow members of the Jockey Club, while in his fine mansion on the most fashionable thoroughfare in London, overlooking Green Park, he could indulge himself in lechery, and give free rein to his all but insatiable virility.

A small, lithe man he was endowed with a cast of countenance hardly calculated to facilitate his perpetual pursuit of dalliance. He had a long oval face, a hooked nose which would become increasingly aquiline with the passing of the years, and small dark eyes. Always fastidiously dressed, he was unlike so many voluptuaries in that he abhorred bawdy stories and loathed coarse language. Whether the object of his assiduous attentions was a countess or a courtesan Old Q's manners were immaculate, although he held out any inducement to obtain entry to a bed, save marriage.

William Douglas, fourth and last Duke of Queensberry, had one of the most honoured names in Scotland, without doing anything whatsoever to enhance it. He was the son of the second Earl of March, and great-grandson of the first Duke of Queensberry, who had been raised to the highest rank in the peerage while serving King Charles II as Lord High Treasurer of Scotland in 1684. The eldest son of the first Duke duly succeeded as second Duke. He was known as 'The Union Duke' on account of his contribution to the amalgamation of the Parliaments of England and Scotland. While a younger son, the grandfather of Old Q, was created Earl of March in 1697. The eldest son of the second Duke was 'The Cannibalistic Idiot'. Unwisely left without supervision during the riots against Union in Edinburgh, he made his way to the servants' quarters, murdered a kitchen boy and roasted the body on a spit. That ogre died in 1715, and his younger brother succeeded as Third Duke of Queensberry.

As William Douglas was only five years of age when he became Third Earl of March on the death of his father in 1731, he was brought up by his mother, the Countess of Ruglen in her own right, who looked forward to him making an appropriate marriage, and settling down to a useful life in Edinburgh. She was to be badly disappointed. The capital of Scotland was far too provincial for the liking of the young Earl of March, who was hardly beyond boyhood before he began yearning for the very much more sophisticated delights of London. Despite his lineage, he felt no affinity at all with Scotland.

As soon as he came of age, Lord March took his departure for London. He had enough money to establish himself in some comfort in Mayfair, and was able to supplement his income by playing, and not infrequently cheating, at cards in White's and the other fashionable clubs around St James's. All the same he lacked the means to indulge in racing, philandering and other forms of pleasure to anything like the extent that he would so dearly liked to have been able to do.

His only hope of putting his finances on the footing he thought they ought to be, lay in his succeeding his father's first cousin the Third Duke of Queensberry, and inheriting the bulk of the family fortune. The trouble from William's point of view, was that the Duke had two sons, albeit as yet unmarried, Henry, Earl of Drumlanrig and Lord Charles Douglas. However, Lord Drumlanrig, was a soldier, whose life was constantly endangered on active service, and his younger brother was consumptive.

In these circumstances William could allow himself to be fairly optimistic about his prospects, until they became decidedly more remote on the marriage of the Earl of Drumlanrig to Lady Mary Hope, the eighteen year old daughter of the Earl of Hopetoun in July 1754. Three months later Lord Drumlanrig was killed in a shooting accident, which was never fully explained and may have been suicide, and in 1756 his younger brother succumbed to consumption. Their father remained heartbroken until he died at the age of eighty in 1778, when the shrewdest gambler and most accomplished seducer in the kingdom

10

became the Fourth Duke of Queensberry. William Wordsworth had recourse to no poetic license when he wrote, "Degenerate Douglas, oh, the unworthy lord!"

Together with Sir Francis Dashwood and George Selwyn, Old Q numbered amongst his most intimate friends John Montagu, Fourth Earl of Sandwich, a flagellant, with a penchant for defloration. It was the Earl who said to John Wilkes, the radical orator, "You, Wilkes, will either die of the pox, or on the gallows."

"That", replied Wilkes, "depends on whether I embrace your lordship's mistress or your lordship's principles."

* * *

Michael Tanner has been specially commissioned to write this account of the racing career of the Duke of Queensberry. Racing was was still in its formative stage and matches, often over a gruelling six miles, between horses belonging to two high betting owners, were very much the order of the day.

* * *

William Douglas, the Fourth Duke of Queensberry, was a living breathing tribute to hedonism. Wine, women and song filled his life. That is when he was not on a racecourse taking money from friend and foe alike, thanks to the Midas touch he exercised in the match races which constituted staple fare on the eighteenth century Turf. Many a time Old Q partnered his own horses in these matches, but on other occasions his jockey Richard Goodisson - 'Hell Fire Dick' to the public - was in the pigskin.

Born on November 5 (a birthday shared with Lester Piggott) 1724, Old Q became the Earl of March upon attaining his majority and inherited the dukedom in 1778 on the death of his first cousin once removed, Charles, the Third Duke of Queensberry. Even as a schoolboy William Douglas was famed for his escapades, a notoriety which followed him to the grave. If anything his behaviour grew more rakish with age as he slipped into what amounted to a second childhood.

An intimate of the Prince of Wales he enjoyed all of Prinny's vices - and more. When not attending meetings of the infamous Hell-Fire Club

11

which regularly satiated its dissolute whims at Medmenham Abbey, near High Wycombe, the home of founder member Sir Francis Dashwood, William Douglas frequented the London gaming clubs, patronised the opera, downed vast quantities of Tokay (a ridiculously expensive Hungarian wine), bathed in warm milk scented with almond powder and ogled every female who passed his house in Piccadilly. "He was," comented one contemporary diarist, "a little, sharp-looking man, very irritable, and he swore like ten thousand troopers." Both Wordsworth and Burns denounced his depredations in verse, while cartoonists depicted him as the "Piccadilly Ambulator" or "The Old Goat of Piccadilly, a shining Star in the British Peerage and a useful Ornament to Society."

Old Q partially compensated for these odious shortcomings with numerous examples of philanthropy (to disabled seamen and refugees from the French Revolution) but the roguish streak lining his soul was guaranteed to manifest itself when offered a profitable outlet in the raffish world of the Turf.

As a young man, Old Q comfortably managed ten stone, complete with saddle, and the Racing Calendar duly records his victories aboard Whipper-in and Smoker as early as the summer of 1748. During the second Newmarket Spring Meeting of 1757, he took part in a memorable match race with the Duke of Hamilton for 1000 guineas in which he displayed superb horsemanship to snatch the spoils.

Making the right match was as much of an art as riding the match. Old Q celebrated the succession to his Dukedom in 1778 by winning matches with Hydaspes, Rocket and Rosalba, in addition to Plates at Newmarket, Huntingdon, Peterborough and Thetford with his best horse, Slim. During the Newmarket season of 1789, he arranged four matches for his horse Dash. At the First Spring Meeting Dash at 6st. 7lb. faced Lord Derby's Derby winner, Sir Peter Teazle at 9st. over six miles for 1000 guineas; at the Second Spring Meeting Dash met a Highflyer colt of Mr Hallam's for 1000 guineas over four miles of the Beacon Course at 8st. 7lb. apiece. At the Second October Meeting he met the Prince of Wales's Don Quixote over six miles for 900 guineas (8st. 7lb.); and a fortnight later the Duke's faithful servant endured three circuits of the Round Course - very nearly twelve miles - against Lord Barrymore's Highlander for 800 guineas again at 8st. 7lb.. Dash won the lot. Just to rub it in, Old Q also matched Mulberry against Sir Peter Teazle conceeding 35lb. over four miles and collected another 500 guineas from Lord Derby. 4200 guineas (£1,600,000) in six months was a tidy haul and a remarkable testimony to Old Q's acumen in matters of the Turf. "He was as dangerous as he was distinguished," observed 'Thormanby', "for no one could touch him in judgment, stable-cunning and jockey-craft."

'Hell-fire Dick' was not exactly an angel either. He was a Yorkshireman of rough and ready habits who, as his soubriquet implies, rode racehorses in the same uncompromising manner. In truth, he and his master were peas from the same pod, opposite ends of the pod perhaps, but the same pod nonetheless.

So, when it came to the crunch, the jockey could not bring himself to betray his benefactor. Goodisson told Old Q that he had been offered a large sum of money to "throw the Duke over," in the forthcoming race. Queensberry listened intently. Accept the money, he declared, "and do not breath a word of this conversation to anyone."

On the day on the race the bookmakers or blacklegs as they were commonly called in those days, laid heavily against the Duke's horse, confident in the knowledge that Goodisson was safely in their pocket. Then, just as Goodisson was about to be legged into the saddle, Old Q tapped him on the shoulder and shouted for all to hear: "Stop! Dick. This is a nice handy nag to ride. I'll get up myself just for the fun of the thing." With that he threw off his coat to reveal the well-known brown Queensberry silks, vaulted into the pigskin and proceeded, naturally, to win the race in a canter. The plot had been foiled; the layers floored.

Old Q died on December 23rd, 1810, aged 86, still unmarried and worth in excess of £1 million (£350,000,000). For Dick Goodisson there was a legacy of £2000 (£750,000). As he grew more infirm he always had within call his French medical attendant, the Pere Elisee, formerly physician to Louis XV, to whom he allowed liberal expenses for every day during which he lived, but nothing more once he was dead.

Few got the better of Old Q, the master of one-up-manship.

* * *

Conclusion by R.O.: The Duke of Queensberry continued to race until he was a very old man. He had his last runner, an un-named four-year-old bay colt by Competitor in a race run in two-and-a-half mile heats at Royal Ascot on 21st June 1805, four months before the battle of Trafalgar. The colt finished third of four to Nitre, a grey mare owned by the Prince of Wales, in the first heat and was then withdrawn - a tame end to a spectacular career on the Turf.

Although cosmopolitan in his tastes, Old Q had a pronounced predilection for ballerinas and opera singers. The number of bastards who could be placed to his credit is necessarily unknown, but the only one in whom he took any noticeable interest was Maria Emily Fagniani. The mother of the child was an Italian diva. Gently born, and a natural harlot, that lady had commenced life as Donna Constanza Brusati. Dark and petite, she materially improved her status by marriage to the Marchese Giacomo Fangiani, heir to one of greatest fortunes in Milan. The Marchese and Marchesa came to England in the company of Henry Montgomery, Earl of Pembroke. While the Marchese lost heavily at the gaming tables of Mayfair, Lord Pembroke enjoyed the pleasures made readily available by the generous disposition of the Marchesa, until passing her on to his friend William Douglas, still Earl of March. On 24th August 1771 Maria Emily, always known as Mie-Mie, was born. Discarding his responsibilities with characteristic nonchalance, the father made her the ward of his friend George Selwyn, by then an ageing bachelor, who absolutely doted on the precocious little girl.

Unfortunately, Mie-Mie grew up to be selfish, petulant, greedy and, as a true daughter of both parents, sexually promiscuous. She was tall and slim, with good features, apart from the rather too prominent nose inherited from her father, but with the large, alluring eyes of her mother. Susceptible to superficial attractions as usual, her father started to show an avuncular interest in Mie-Mie as she came to womanhood, and arranged for her to marry the Earl of Yarmouth, whose prospects made him acceptable despite his depravity, as he was heir to the enormous fortune of his father, Francis Seymour-Conway, second Marquess of Hertford.

Old Q may have been well pleased with the match but the Seymour-Conway family was not. Haughtily they subjected the natural daughter of the Scottish Duke to every kind of slight and insult, with the result that Mie-Mie persuaded her husband to take her to live in France. It was in Paris, therefore, that she brought up her two sons; Richard, who acquired the courtesy title of Earl of Yarmouth upon the death of his grandfather in 1822, and Lord Henry Seymour.

The paternity of Lord Henry Seymour was a matter of much interest and speculation. The general concensus of opinion was that his father was the Comte de Montrond. The son of a landowner in Franche-Compte, Montrond was an accomplished swordsman with a taste for heavy gambling, whose talent for duplicity rendered him invaluable as a spy in the service of the Foreign Minister, the Prince de Talleyrand. Nevertheless, despite the strong resemblance which Lord Henry bore to the Comte de Montrond, many people were convinced that he was the son of Andoche Junot, Duc d'Abrantes, the favourite *aide-de-campe* of the Emperor Napoleon.

Only too well aware that he would receive no welcome from his supposed Conway-Seymour relatives in England, Lord Henry decided to spend his life in France. With his crude sense of humour, which which gave him a penchant for tasteless practical jokes, and a proclivity for brawling in the boulevards after bouts of heavy drinking, Lord Henry was in his element amongst the aristocratic riff-raff, who became the leaders of Parisian society after the restoration of the Legitimist Monarchy in the person of Louis XVIII in 1815.

Although reconciled to exile, Lord Henry cultivated a number of decidedly English tastes, notably horseracing, which he introduced into France. In addition, he used part of the fortune he had inherited from his maternal grandfather, the Duke of Queensberry, to lay the foundations of the French Stud Book, by the importation of Ibrahim, winner of the Two Thousand Guineas in 1835, and other high class horses. In 1833 he became the first President of the French Jockey Club, and for a number of years had a string of some thirty horses in training with Tom Carter, who had two younger Englishmen, the brothers Tom and Henry Jennings, as his assistants. In due course Tom Jennings had the Phantom House stable, now the quarters of William Jarvis, where he became responsible for Gladiateur being the first French-bred winner of the Derby in 1865.

For a time Lord Henry's stable dominated French racing. He won the first running of the French Derby with Franck in 1836, and he won it again with Lydia in 1837, Vendredi in 1838 and for a fourth time with Poetess. Unfortunately the many deficiencies in a character deeply flawed by heredity, included an inability to lose gracefully. When the horses of the likes of Auguste Lupin, Eugene Aumont and Prince Marc de Beauvais began to be as successful as his his own, Lord Henry rapidly became disillusioned with racing. He had his last runner on 5th June 1842, and seventeen days later he sold off all his horses. The youthful libertine was already fast becoming the dissolute middle-aged Lothario, who treated his mistresses shamefully. Soon his eyesight was failing, and he was only aged fifty-four when he died of anthrax in 1859. Thus Old Q's grandson was the Englishman who never set foot in England and introduced horse racing to France.

So far as morality was concerned, Mie-Mie's elder son Richard, blessed by legitimacy, was no improvement whatever on Lord Henry, although he was to be responsible for the nation receiving a quite priceless inheritance. As lecherous as his grandfather, and as licentious as his mother, he was only eighteen when he became the father of a boy by a Mrs. Jackson, a comely Scotswoman, a good few years older than himself, whom he met at Brighton. Born Miss Wallace, she was the wife of a serving officer in the army

On the death of his father in 1842, Richard Seymour became the fourth Marquis of Hertford, and the possessor of a rent-roll of £100,000 a year. Notwithstanding the deplorable deficiencies in his personality, none of which precluded his investiture with the Order of the Garter, he was a man of remarkably cultivated taste. On entering upon his vast inheritance, Lord Hertford set about buying fine paintings and other *objets d'art*. His agents were in constant negotiation for those in private ownership, and while in company with a handsome, well set-up young man with a black walrus moustache whose advice he valued highly, Lord Hertford toured galleries and exhibitions indefatigably. His companion was the result of his youthful liaison in Brighton. Originally called Richard Jackson, he became known as Richard Wallace, as it was felt more seemly that he should bear the maiden name of his mother, rather than that of her badly cuckolded husband.

16

The Fourth Marquis of Hertford died in 1870, without legitimate issue. Being well aware of the contempt in which the rest of the Seymour family held the sons of Mie-Mie, he left no more than the estates in England and Ireland, together with the rest of the entailed property, to his successor in the title, General Francis Seymour a distant cousin, descended from the First Marquis, and one time equerry to the Prince Consort, who most certainly would not have approved of Mie-Mie. The rest of his huge fortune and, more importantly, his now priceless collection, of art, Lord Hertford bequeathed to his natural son Richard Wallace.

Badly belying his blood, Richard Wallace acquired quite faultless respectability. He sat as Member of Parliament for Lisburn from 1873 to 1875, received a Baronetcy, and was a trustee of both the National Gallery and the National Portrait Gallery. When Sir Richard Wallace died in 1890 all his cherished treasures were inherited by his wife. Although Lady Wallace was French by birth, being originally Julie Amelie Charlotte Castelnau, she honoured what she knew to be the wishes of her husband, by leaving the magnificent collection of fine art, which he had greatly augmented, to the English nation on her death in 1897.

As one surveys the glories of the Wallace Collection in Hertford House in Manchester Square, in the angle of Baker Street and Wigmore Street, it is pleasant to contemplate its origin. It was a gift from the illegitimate son of the Fourth Marquis of Hertford, who in turn was the son of the illegitimate daughter of the Fourth and last Duke of Queensberry. The art of the Tart.

During the time that Mie-Mie was bringing up her sons, her father was refusing to be reconciled with old age. By the turn of the century in 1800, the year that Alessandro Volta invented the first electric battery and Napoleon crushed Austria at Marengo, Old Q was seventy five years old and his lust was quite undiminished.

He had already taken leave of Newmarket, to spend his declining years in London, where people making their way down Piccadilly, would see a wizened little old man with a hooked nose, sitting on the balcony of his house with a glass in his hand, ogling anything in a skirt. For many years the old rascal had been known as the wickedest man in England. Now he was simply "The Star of Piccadilly," and, as such,

17

celebrated in verse, following one of several premature reports of his demise. Among the verses of that decorous, albeit untimely, requiem were the following:

> *And what is all this grand to-do*
> *That runs each street and alley through?*
> *Tis the departure of "Old Q",*
> *The Star of Piccadilly.*

> *"Thank Heaven! Thank Heaven! " Exclaims Miss Prue*
> *"My mother, and grandmother too,*
> *Can now walk safe from that vile Q"*
> *The Star of Piccadilly.*

> *The jockey boys, Newmarket's crew,*
> *Who know a little thing - or two,*
> *Cry out "He's done! we've done Old Q"*
> *The Star of Piccadilly.*

> *Poll, Peggy, Cath'rine, Patty, Sue,*
> *Descendants of old dames he knew,*
> *All mourn your tutor, Ancient Q,*
> *The Star of Piccadilly.*

> *Old Nick he whisked his tail so blue,*
> *And grinn'd, and leer'd, and look'd askew,*
> *"Oh ho" he said "I've got my Q!"*
> *The Star of Piccadilly .*

Whether Old Nick did take him, or whether belated repentance obtained for him more comfortable accommodation, the tryst was made on 23rd December 1810.

Two reminders of Old Q are still to be seen at Newmarket. Entering the town from the direction of Cambridge, you can see on your right Queensberry House, a fine red brick building and now the headquarters of the British Bloodstock Agency. On the opposite side of the High Street is Queensberry Lodge, a delightful little white cottage, redolent with history, and behind it the disused stableyard in which 'Chubb'

Leach trained with such success from 1931 until 1953. In earlier times it had been the quarters of John Dawson the younger, and other well known trainers of the nineteenth century

*   *   *

Michael Tanner is a distinguished Turf historian and a pioneer of sectional, furlong by furlong, timing of races. Among the notable books which he has written are *The King George VI Chase* (1984), *Great Racing Partnerships* (The Sportman's Press, 1987), *The Champion Hurdle* (Pelham Books, 1989) and *Great Jockeys of the Flat* (Guinness Publishing, 1992). In addition he contributes to *The Sporting Life, The Racing Post, The Sporting Life Weekender, Horse and Hound, Pacemaker International,* and, until its closure in 1989, *The European Racehorse.*

Born in Oxford in 1947, Michael attended a local grammar school, prior to going to St Edmund's Hall, Oxford, where he obtained a BA (Hons) Degree in Geography. He has played rugby for both Oxfordshire and Leicestershire.

Before becoming a freelance racing journalist, he was a schoolmaster for eighteen years. He lives in Lincolnshire with his wife and two daughters.

A SURPRISE ARRIVAL AT DONCASTER

(Lord George Bentinck's 1836 St Leger Winner)

Introduction by R.O.: So far as the bookmakers were concerned, Lord George Bentinck had mastered the mysteries of bilocation, the ability to be in two places simultaneously, when he produced Elis at Doncaster in time to run in the St. Leger of 1836. According to their information, then, as now, almost uncannily reliable, the colt was in his box in the Goodwood stable, on the Duke of Richmond's Sussex estate, 240 miles to the South. Not for the first time, though, they had badly underestimated the resourcefulness of Lord George, and it was going to cost them dear.

By any standards, the talents of Lord George were formidable. Allied to a natural air of authority, was great organisational ability. He was energetic, had the intellect to appreciate the essence of a problem rapidly, and vision. On the other hand he was arrogant, vindictive, quarrelsome and devious. He was also totally humourless. During his brief service with the Ninth Royal Lancers he returned to Chatham Barracks after dinner to find his room filled with stray dogs, chickens and a goat. He did not take the joke in good part, regarding it as evidence of the lack of proper respect by the perpetrators for the son of a Duke.

As well as being intensely unpopular with his brother cornets, Lord George, tall and undeniably handsome, infuriated senior officers by his barely concealed insolence and almost casual attitude to his responsibilities. Finally, his immediate superior, Captain Ker, who was both conscientious and well liked, sent him a letter enumerating the duties he was to perform as punishment for behaviour which was regarded as prejudicial to regimental morale. Rather than accept the rebuke, Lord George demanded an investigation. The Court of Inquiry was held on 10th February 1821 to consider allegations of inattention

21

to duty as well as contemptuous, insubordinate and disrespectful behaviour. On Ker failing to prove his case, the Court found in favour of Cornet Lord George Bentinck, who was still seventeen days short of his nineteenth birthday, and the Captain was obliged to apologise, while seething at being bettered by his haughty insubordinate. Shortly afterwards, Bentinck went to Paris. Ker followed him, and challenged him to a duel in the Bois de Boulogne, but one of Lord George's more influential relatives got wind of the affair, and arranged for the French police to arrive on the scene to prevent the encounter from taking place.

As Lord George was every bit as objectionable to his fellow owners, as he had been to the officers of the Ninth Royal Lancers, Captain Ker was certainly not the only man to call him out to a duel. In September of 1835, Lord George was staying with the Earl of Wilton at Heaton Park, near Manchester, for the three-day race meeting staged in the grounds. The lines on which that fixture was conducted were by no means to the liking of everybody, as the handicapper was always invited to join the house party, and by way of appreciation of the hospitality, was expected to treat the horses owned by Lord Wilton and his guests favourably.

Determined to defeat the system and knowing that Irish form was held in very low regard, George Osbaldeston, the peppery little Yorkshire squire, bought a horse called Rush, who had won two or three Oueen's Plates in Ireland.

After Rush, owner up, had finished last of four to Lady de Gros, who was giving him a stone, on the first day, the Squire entered him for the Gold Cup, for which the weights were compiled overnight, to be run the following day. On the strength of his indifferent showing behind Lady de Gros, Rush was set to receive another stone from her. The betting was very heavy indeed, with George Payne, of Sulby Abbey, Northamptonshire, one of the most fearless punters of the day, backing Rush to win several thousand pounds at 10-1, and Osbaldeston also supporting his horse substantially. For his part Lord George laid against Rush, who wound up a strong favourite at 2-1.

Going down to the post, the Squire rode up to the judge, who had shown an obvious partiality for Lord Wilton's horses, and said, "Take a good look at these colours, as you will need to remember them". He was right. Rush won easily from Lady de Gros. Lord George was furious convinced that the horse had not been allowed to run on his merits in the first race, in order to obtain more lenient treatment in the second.

Settlement of the bets struck at Heaton Park, and elsewhere the previous week was made at the Hyde Park Corner premises of Messrs. Tattersalls the following Monday, in accordance with long established custom. Lord George made no attempt to pay the £400 (£68,000) he owed Osbaldeston over Rush. On being approached by the Squire, he replied, "Do you mean say, Sir, that you dare to ask me for the money for that robbery? For it was robbery, and you know it!".

Osbaldeston, therefore, demanded an apology for the insinuation of cheating, together with payment of the money due, or satisfaction on the Field of Honour. Lord George, true to his own nature, if nothing else, refused to retract a word, and accepted the challenge to a duel with pistols.

The outcome could only be regarded as a foregone conclusion. Lord George was a dead man. Squire Osbaldeston was a marksman and widely regarded as the finest shot in the Kingdom. The mutual friends of the antagonists were horrified. Osbaldeston experienced the greatest difficuly in finding a second, while friends of Lord George begged him to offer an apology, or at least ameliorate his allegations. Lord George was proudly impervious to all approaches, and appointed Colonel George Anson as his second.

Lord George and Squire Osbaldeston met at six o'clock in the morning at Wormwood Scrubs. Before pistols were loaded, Colonel Anson warned them that if either killed the other, the survivor would face a charge of murder, and then ordered them to fire on his count of three.

"One" he called out, and after an unexpectedly long pause, "two", followed by "three", in almost the same breath. Completely taken aback by the unexpectedly rapid completion of the count, Lord George fired into the air, while Squire Osbaldeston took careful aim - and fired his ball straight through Lord George's hat. The seconds declared themselves satisfied, and in accordance with the etiquette of duelling, that was the end of the matter.

George Anson became commander-in-chief in India. While at dinner one evening in 1857, a servant brought him a telegram. Thinking it discourteous to open it in front of his guests, he put it in his pocket. His exquisite manners cost valuable time. The wire announced the outbreak of the mutiny. Shortly afterwards Anson died of cholera.

The way in which Lord George treated social equals necessarily gave rise to great offence, but far more reprehensible was his use of his authority and influence to bring about the downfall of humbler folk who had earned his displeasure. For reasons long forgotten he conceived a deep hatred of John Orton, who acted as judge and clerk of the course at York, and declared he would never run a horse on the Knavesmire, while Orton retained either office. To their eternal discredit, the members of the the Race Committee placated Lord George by dismissing Orton, shortly after he had been responsible for the inauguration of the Ebor Handicap in 1843, and within a matter of months the poor man was dead.

Lord George Bentinck may have brought a great many benefits to racing, by ridding it of defaulters, corrupt jockeys and other undesirable characters, as well achieving much by way of increasing the efficiency with which meetings were conducted, but in all too many cases, he treated people abominably. Moreover, the methods which he employed to bring off his enormous bets were often questionable, and did little credit to a member of the Jockey Club.

*　　*　　*

George Ennor shows that Lord George Bentinck did not always need recourse to deception to land his coups. Pure ingenuity enabled him to deal the ring a heavy blow, when he won the St. Leger with Elis in 1836.

*　　*　　*

In that self-righteous way so typical of their genre, politicians have decided that what they call insider trading in the world of finance should be a criminal offence. Quite why it should be a crime to take advantage of what you know when someone else does not have the same information has never really been made clear, and happily no-one has ever tried to impose such a ruling in the world of racing and betting.

24

Everyone likes to think that he or she may know a bit more about a horse than others; knowledge of what a horse may have achieved on home gallops can provide a vital edge when it comes to making an investment and correspondingly the bookmakers' intelligence service is often able to pick up stories, sometimes accurate and sometimes wishful thinking, about any particular state of play.

Thus was the case shortly before the St. Leger of 1836, for which Lord George Bentinck's colt Elis, who had been runner-up in the Two Thousand Guineas to the subsequent Derby winner Bay Middleton, would have been a major fancy had it been certain that he was going to take part. The bookmakers, though, were so certain that Elis would not run at Doncaster that they offered much longer odds against him than they would have done had the colt's participation been assured.

The reason for the bookmakers' enthusiasm to lay the colt was the direct result of their intelligence service, although by modern standards it seems strange that if they continued to offer overly generous odds about Elis no-one smelled a rat and wondered why they were doing so.

The pencillers, though, had good reason to think that they were "laying a stiff' un". In those days the only way for a horse to travel from either his home base or from one racecourse to another was to walk. There were no such things as horseboxes and though steam trains had been running for about fifteen years, they were still very much in their infancy.

Everyone knew that the time required from Goodwood, where Elis had been completing what was presumed to be his St. Leger preparation under the eye of John Kent senior, to get to Doncaster was fifteen days, so when Elis was still in Sussex the week before the St. Leger the bookmakers were entitled to have every confidence in laying him up and down the book.

They did so in ignorance of the plans of Elis' owner. Though the colt ran in the name of Lord Lichfield, he in fact belonged to Lord George Bentinck who raced the colt in Lichfield's name in order to persuade his father, the Duke of Portland, that he was not becoming too involved in racing and betting.

Bentinck has rightly acquired the reputation of being one of those mostly responsible for reforming the conduct and administration of racing and for trying to stamp out the villainy with which the sport had become almost fatally infected during the early part of the Nineteenth century. It was very largely due to him that the ringing affair of Running Rein and Maccabaeus in the 1844 Derby (see *Volume One of Great Racing Gambles and Frauds*) was exposed and its perpetrators denied what would have been their ill-gotten gains.

But for all that Bentinck was not only an altruist. He was a very heavy gambler when the idea appealed and by no means all of his contemporaries regarded him as without blemish. What credence should be given to the comments of that arch-villain William Day, whose acerbic relationship with Bentinck ended when letters from Day to Bentinck and to a bookmaker were placed in the wrong envelopes, is perhaps not even debatable, though one might wonder why Bentinck was involved with Day in the first place.

A far more reliable witness was Bentinck's one time partner Charles Greville, whose diaries were far from complimentary even after Bentinck's successful exposé of the Ruining Rein scandal and in which he refers to his former confederate's "peculiar code of morality and honour". To what, if indeed any, extent Bentinck offended even Greville over the Elis exercise is far from clear. The only sufferers were the bookmakers and as they were purely and simply outwitted by a better tactician; they had no justifiable cause for complaint even though Bentinck did win a considerable sum from them.

The bookies were right in their opinion that Elis was still at Goodwood in the week before the St. Leger and they were just as right in their view that it would take at least a fortnight to get the colt to Doncaster. What they did not know, however, was that Lord George was poised to embark on an idea which would in due course revolutionise the means of moving horses about the country.

Lord George remembered a horse being transported from Worcestershire to Newmarket in a bullock van and decided that a similar vehicle on the Goodwood estate could be adapted for the same purpose. He employed a coach builder named Herring, whose works were in Long Acre near what used to be Covent Garden fruit market, to build a van of similar style capable of carrying two horses. As might have been expected, Bentinck did not tell Herring why he needed the van and its very existence was kept as secret as possible.

Once the van was constructed to his satisfaction, Bentinck continued

26

to take every precaution for the horses' (Elis' regular workmate The Drummer was also travelling) journey and told John Kent that only corn and hay from Goodwood should be taken and that even the sieve from which Elis ate had to come from there.

Elis, who clearly had a very placid nature allied with his tough constitution - he had recently had four races in two-and-a-half weeks, including the two-and-a-half mile Goodwood Cup - was loaded into the van with no difficulty and with six post horses driven by John Doe, who seems to have been some sort of assistant to John Kent, pulling it, the van set off on its historic journey.

According to the memoirs of John Kent junior, the son of Elis' trainer, people in the villages and towns it passed through were amazed at the sight and their theories about it ranged from the transport of an exceptionally fierce animal, to the move to trial of some particularly infamous villain. When it was necessary to change horses there were sometimes only two pairs available or necessary but the journey, which was split into three daily sections of about eighty miles, was accomplished with the minimum of difficulty.

En route, a somewhat indirect route it appears, the horses were disembarked and galloped on the racecourse at Lichfield (there is no record that Elis' alleged owner may also have owned the course) before arriving at Doncaster on the Monday before the race. Elis walked with a total lack of concern to his stable and after he and The Drummer had galloped on the course the following morning, the once so readily available 12-1 had long since disappeared.

John Kent junior wrote that the two horses arrived at Doncaster on the Monday, which was "two days before The St. Leger". Obviously Kent, writing more than fifty years later, muddled his days as the St. Leger was run on Tuesday 20th September in 1836. It certainly seems a bit strange that if Elis and The Drummer galloped at Lichfield on the Sunday they did not leave there for another twenty four hours. The horsebox must have reached Doncaster on the Sunday evening.

It was, according to Kent, "generally remarked" (by those who saw Elis at Doncaster before the race) "that although he came into Doncaster in the rear of six horses, he will leave twice that number to inspect his tail in the great race".

Thirteen lined up against Elis, who went off as second favourite at 7-1.

The Malton trained Scroggins, owned and ridden by William Scott and trained by his brother John, was at the head of the market at 6-4 but once John Day, perhaps the most amoral of that villainous family from Danebury, had sent Elis to the front "at the Red House" (approximately where the home turn is now), the exercise had become no contest. Elis won by two lengths "easily" from Scroggins with the filly Beeswing (spelled Bee's Wing by Fletcher), who was later to win the Gold Cup, the Doncaster Cup four times and forty-six other races, a head back in third.

Bentinck had well and truly taken the bookmakers to the cleaners. He had apparently struck a wager of £12,000 to £1,000 (£2,000,000 to £170,000), about the colt when no-one thought that Elis would get to Doncaster and had never thought of the idea of Lord George's new-fangled van. It is questionable which was the bigger gamble, Bentinck's actual bet or the mode of transport in which he placed such faith without the possibility of any stand-by plan. Both came off handsomely.

*   *   *

Conclusion by R.O.: Without doubt, Lord George Bentinck was one of the most able administrators of his generation. Had he devoted his talents to politics, rather than to the Turf for the better part of his life, he would almost certainly have achieved high office, like his grandfather, the Third Duke of Portland (1738-1809), who was Prime Minister from 1807 until his resignation in the year of his death.

As it was, Lord George was Member of Parliament for King's Lynn from the time that he reached the tender age of twenty-four in 1826, but made no noticeable impact on the house for a very long time, frequently attending with hunting pink clearly discernible beneath his overcoat. After twenty years, however, he caused a major sensation by selling off all his bloodstock for £10,000 (£1,700,000), in 1846, in order to devote all his energy to his duties in the Commons. In June of that year the Conservative Prime Minister, Sir Robert Peel, had split his party by repealing the Corn Laws, which had inflated the price of bread by imposing a duty on imported grain, in order to alleviate the famine caused by the failure of the potato crop in Ireland, and the consequences of a series of poor harvests in England. Thus, in 1846, Lord George accepted the leadership of the Protectionist wing of the

Conservative Party with the future Prime Minister Benjamin Disraeli as his principal lieutenant, the main plank of their policy being the defence of the interest of the landowners. Two years later, in 1848, Lord George Bentinck died of a heart attack at the age of forty-six, while on a walk across his father's Welbeck Abbey estate in Nottinghamshire.

The irony of Lord George Bentinck's life was that whereas Sir Robert Peel destroyed his chance of holding ministerial office by driving him into opposition, as leader of the protectionists, the chief beneficiary of Lord George's greatest achievement, the exposure of Running Rein as ringer for the four-year-old Maccabaeus, was the Prime Minister's younger brother General Jonathan Peel. The latter owned Orlando, who was awarded the notorious Derby of 1884, following the inevitable disqualification of Running Rein/Maccabaeus.

* * *

George Ennor was elected President of the Horserace Writers' Association in 1974, and retires from that position in April 1994. During the course of twenty years he has undertaken a huge volume of voluntary work for the benefit of his colleagues, by way of successful negotiation for improved facilities and other amenities on racecourses. Born in 1940, he was educated at Malvern. After two years working for Pratt & Co, stakeholders and managers of the course at Folkestone, Fontwell and Plumpton, he joined *The Sporting Life* in 1960, becoming Senior Reporter in 1984, before joining *The Racing Post* in the same capacity during October of the following year. He also writes for *Daily Racing Form* in the United States, and has contributed to *Horse and Hound, The Bloodstock Breeders' Review,* and *The Johannesburg Star,* as well as *The European Racehorse,* until its demise in 1989.

29

THE WELSHERS TERRORISE BOOKMAKERS AND RACEGOERS

(Violence Runs Rife on the Course in the 1850's)

Introduction by R.O.: Strolling through the ranks of the bookmakers in Tattersalls, looking for a price, the punter needs to give no thought to his safety. The situation was very different little more than one hundred years ago, when a racegoer risked life and limb on all too many courses, and all the achievements of Lord George Bentinck had been undone. Moreover, when he backed a winner, the punter would frequently fail to collect his dues, as he would find that the man who had accepted his stake had decamped, or allege that he had backed another horse, and had two or three very large friends on hand, to provide the necessary testimomy as to that being the case.

Horse racing has never been blighted with a more appalling reputation than it was during the middle of Queen Victoria's reign, in the 'sixties and 'seventies of the last century. Many of the smaller courses were little more than thieves' kitchens. That was particularly true of those in the London area, such as West Drayton, Bromley, Kingsbury and Streatham, and even 'Appy 'Ampton was not always that felicitous. Many of those who stood up, purporting to make a book, were amongst the most depraved members of society, with no intention whatever of paying out over a winner, and were simply intent upon preying on a hopefully gullible public. At the same time violence was widespread, and gangs, many of whom came from the slums of the provincial cities, descended on the capital, roamed the metropolitan courses, robbing relentlessly, without even having recourse to the finesse of the pick-pocket, while the honest bookmakers were the victims of vicious extortion. Every kind of thug and ruffian was in his element on the racecourse, but the ones that plied much the most

31

lucrative trade were the welshers.

*   *   *

In his autobiography *A Wasted Life,* published by Grant Richards in 1902, the Victorian bookmaker *Dyke Wilkinson,* gave a vivid account of the activities of the welshers, and the immense harm they were able to do to horse racing over a number of years during the middle of the last century.

*   *   *

I have often wondered what could be the derivation of the word "welsher" as applied among betting men. I have heard many, but none which has seemed to me perfectly satisfactory. A friend whom I have just consulted on the subject says there is no doubt it was suggested by the old rhyme commencing

" Taffy was a Welshman, Taffy was a thief."

But I am not prepared to accept this derivation either, and am afraid my friend has allowed his judgment to be warped by prejudice, after a prolonged residence in private apartments at a fashionable Welsh watering-place, where they kept a cat, or, I should say, a great many cats. However awkward my readers may find the derivation of the word, a good many of them will experience no difficulty in supplying its definition, for they have had, in the course of their racing experiences, practical illustrations of it. I don't suppose the word welshing has any great antiquity, but the practice is as old as gambling of any sort, and it has not been confined to the turf alone.

A form of welshing was very common 150 years ago, during the insane rage for lotteries. Of course, a good many of these gambling schemes were genuine enough, and among the millions of blanks some were fortunate enough to draw prizes of immense value. But those systems had their blacklegs and welshers. It was no uncommon thing for lottery offices to be opened, and after receiving from great numbers of poor dupes, the managers, as they were called, would do "a guy", just as we have seen the same class act on racecourses in the present day. Sometimes, however, instead of levanting and closing the office in this sudden manner, they would conduct a bogus draw, in which the prizes would be so ridiculously out of proportion to the blanks that they frequently led to riots and sometimes loss of life.

My very earliest personal experience of betting on horseracing has doubtless been the lot of many of my readers. My first acquaintance with a welsher was when a youth—I needn't say how long it is ago. I found myself at a race-meeting. I knew nothing of the horses or jockeys or anything, but I had half-a-crown in my pocket, so made up my mind to invest it, and as the jockeys paraded their horses in front of the Grand Stand, for lack of better judgment I selected the one I considered wore the prettiest jacket, and planked down my half dollar on him. Of course, it was a most silly thing to do, but, as luck would have it, this very horse won at 5 to 1. According to my hazy method of calculation, I made out there was twelve and sixpence coming from the bookie to whom I had confided my half-crown. Don't laugh, gentle reader; I have seen the same mistake made many times since those days by much older and cleverer people. However, I went back gleefully to the spot where I left my bookie and my half-crown; but the bland looking, elderly person, with the black surtout coat and shiny top-hat, was nowhere to be seen. He'd been shouting a good deal, and I thought that probably he was dry and had gone to get a drink, so, unsuspecting guile in such a gentlemanly-looking elderly person, I waited with composure his return; but when I found the numbers up for the next race and the betting in full swing again, I began to think I must have come to the wrong shop, so I moved away in search of my bookie. During my ramble round the outside of the enclosure—on the opposite side to where I had made my bet—I came across a man with a remarkable family likeness to the gentleman, only he was wearing a light jacket with blue stripes and a white hat. Still feeling confident he was my man, I made for him and demanded my twelve and sixpence. He simply said, in an indignant tone:

"Go away, sir ! What do you mean?"

But before I could explain my meaning, I was hustled away by a couple of roughish-looking men.

"Yo've bin welshed, ain't you?" asked one of these gentlemen.

"Well, I don't know what you mean by welshed," I replied; "but I backed the last winner with that gentleman for half-a crown, and I want my money."

"Look 'ere," the man said, "did the joker wot bet wi' yo wear a black coort like a parson, and a shiny black top-hat?" This I was obliged to confess was so. "Theer yer are agen," he said, turning appealingly to his companion; "dain't I tell yer the d—d old thief was at his games agen!" Then turning to me, he continued: "The feller wot did yo is that other gent's brother; yo cum to-morrer an we'll find 'im for yer. Ye mustn't 'inder that gent in is busniss, or yo'll get locked up."

I didn't find it convenient to "cum to-morrer"; indeed, it was a good many years before I was able to attend Wolverhampton—or, for the matter of that, any other—race meeting.

Welshing during my time has had three distinct periods, each marked with characteristics peculiar to itself. From earliest recollections of the turf up to about 1872, welshing was a very mild sort of thing, and its professors were, for the most part, rather elderly men, with a dejected, decidedly seedy and out-of-elbows sort of look about them. I don't believe it was generally so flourishing a sort of business. There was no organised ruffianism, such as we hereafter became so familiar with; indeed, there was no union of any sort among them, consequently little strength. When one of these mean sneaks secured a few pounds he was only too anxious to be off with it, thinking himself lucky if he escaped a cruel pummelling at the hands of an enraged crowd or a ducking in the nearest water.

They were mostly a quiet, inoffensive set of men, and but for their thieving propensities, quite harmless.

I think my next experience of racing will illustrate pretty correctly the character of these old-fashioned welshers. My friend Collins had supplied me with an infallible method of backing horses which was to produce untold wealth, and a ring full of broken bookmakers.

I will not repeat how this marvellous system terminated, but looking round about Upper Norwood, East Molesey, Edgbaston, and, indeed, many of the genteel suburbs of London, and most of our great cities, it is easy to gather evidence that the portion of my dreams relating to the bookies is still some little distance off fulfilment. As my readers are aware, it was at glorious Goodwood I made my *début* as a backer. For the first three or four races no favourite won, so my system now called upon me to take 40 to 20 a horse whose name I have forgotten. The bookie I had done my business with so far was rather a meek-looking little fellow, very quiet—I liked him for that. He wasn't much of a swell to look at. I didn't object to that either, knowing so many substantial people affected a seediness in attire; he was dressed in a well-worn suit of black, giving him rather more the appearance of an underpaid curate, minus the white choker, than a common betting man. This also pleased me, so I handed him four nice new fivers, and when, a few minutes afterwards, my horse had won, I ran off the stand with my friend, eager to touch my first winnings. On my way I said to my friend:

"What a nice little fellow that is we've been betting with— so very civil and obliging!"

"Yes, he is very civil," answered my friend; " but you must remember we have done nothing but lose to him so far, and it's easy for anyone to be civil when they are winning your money."

"Ah! You—you'll find him quite as agreeable now he has to pay," I replied. "But where is the gentleman? That's his place against that pillar. Another gentleman seems to have taken up his position." Then, thinking of my Wolverhampton experience, I felt a sinking sensation come over me. I didn't for a moment imagine my quiet little friend was a vulgar welsher; but began to think, after previous experience, I was a bit of a fool not to have taken steps to assure myself of the stability of my bookie before I began betting with him. However, we waited, and he didn't turn up; we searched for him, and couldn't find him; so we began to make inquiries, and found that he was a notorious old welsher named Manning, then, in all probability, on his way back to town to enjoy himself with the unusually large and easily got plunder of a couple of young fools.

This last experience sufficed for the remainder of my life. It is true I have been welshed many times, and for very large amounts, since those days, but not by the common welsher.

Some two months after this incident I went with my friend, the theory inventor, and some other acquaintances, to Warwick Races, and on alighting on the platform at the Great Western Station, the first person I set eyes on was the meek-looking Mr. Manning, with the same seedy suit of black and melancholy visage. I and my friends surrounded him, demanding the sixty pounds. The little gentleman looked somewhat alarmed, but he affected immense surprise.

"What do you want sixty pounds of me for, gentlemen?" he meekly inquired.

"What you welshed me of at Goodwood," I replied. "Come, no nonsense; pull it out!"

"Goodwood!, young man, you are quite mistaken. I'll take my solemn oath I never was at Goodwood in all my life."

And then he called upon the Almighty, in the most choice and powerful language, to bear witness to his truth; also to afflict him with all sorts of horrors if he had ever been near Goodwood, or knew where it was. He was a cowardly little villain, and trembled with fear, doubtless possessed with a lively recollection of some previous rough handlings by other victims. Well, what could we do with him? It was clear he was the man, but it was equally clear he had scarcely sixty pence, much less sixty pounds, about him. And no amount of punishment we could inflict would get any of my money back. So I was weak enough to believe I was proposing something clever when I said:

"Now look here, Manning, old fellow, I know all about you, and if you don't make a clean breast of it, confessing you're the man, and also promising to pay me a bit at a time, as you may be able to, we'll take you down to yonder pool of stagnant water and duck you within an inch of your life."

Of course, he confessed instantly, and promised all I asked, and much more. What would he not have done to get clear of us at that moment? And he snivelled in most abject fashion over my weakness, which he was cunning enough to call kindness. I saw a good deal of the poor old wretch in after years, but need scarcely say didn't get a penny of the sixty pounds. I rather think he whispered me occasionally for bits of silver to help him home after some of his unsuccessful excursions, presuming, no doubt, on his very early connection with my racing career. I haven't seen poor old Joe now for many years, but suppose he has gone the way of so many better men with whom I became acquainted in my early racing days, and who still hold a place in my memory.

As far as observation goes, I don't think many of the "chosen people" have gone astray in this direction—for these wary gentlemen the game was never good enough—but I am sorry to record the fact that I remember one welsher, and I daresay there are some old racing men who will remember him better than I do. He was a big dark man, with a most pronounced Semitic cast of face, and a stoop in his shoulders; the appearance of having in some part of his life lost something he was for ever seeking to find. Like his friend and contemporary, Manning, he wore a quiet, almost sad expression, perhaps not the most desirable, yet one of the endurable parasites of racing. He was called " big Nathan."

An equally well-known old traveller in the same line was poor old Johnny Quin. I have frequently heard him called "the honest welsher," I suppose the adjective being used here in the comparative sense. It was not that he refrained from plunder where he had the opportunity, or that he was ever known, willingly, to repay the victims he had robbed; but I have known highly respectable members of the ring lend him half-a-sovereign to go to a race-meeting or to help him home again after an unsuccessful meeting, and these amounts he never failed to repay. One good-hearted—albeit, perhaps indiscreet—bookie, who was frequently Johnny's banker, was soundly abused for this practice.

"Ah well, we've all to live," he would say, "so has this poor old devil; he lives on the involuntary contributions of the new 'mugs.' How many of us are doing the same in a different way ? Good luck to him!"

I have said that these old-fashioned welshers were almost a harmless set of men. Compared with the class which succeeded them, they were honest gentlemen. They were mostly very poor, and I have often thought they were welshers less from choice than necessity.

The most notable example of the class I have hitherto written of was a man known for many years as "the Captain", and by this name only shall he be known here, not only because he lived to occupy a far different position on the turf and in commercial life, but because he has left behind him some who inherit only the better traits of his character and the worthiest traditions of his life. Of this singular type of his class I shall now have to speak.

The Captain was known wherever there was racing all over England, and, taking him altogether, his was the most interesting personality which has ever appeared on the turf in the shape of a welsher. In

37

personal appearance he was a remarkable man; he was thick-set and rather above the average height; his face, although badly pock-marked, indicated considerable shrewdness and natural intelligence; his eyes, small keen, and restless like those of a bird of prey, were always on the lookout for victims; he wore his iron-grey hair cropped short as with a clipping machine; he made up for this, however, by cultivating a splendid moustache of the same colour. In his bearing he affected the high military style of which he was uncommonly proud, and which, doubtless, had secured him his nick-name. In his manners he was suave and gentle, and polite almost to excess, and he exercised, in the practice of his despicable calling, a patient perseverance, industry, and ability which—applied in a more legitimate course—might have secured him a big position in life. As it was, they got for him several rows of houses, and with them a certain sort of consideration and respect, which the world always concedes to wealth, or reputed wealth, and to success—however achieved.

The Captain was, indeed, the only one of the welshers belonging to his school who got money and saved it; to begin with, he had more ability than his fellows, and what, even more than this, accounted for it, was the fact of his being a steady, sober sort of fellow, with the one fixed idea, never to "part"—for any purpose, or to any person—when he had once secured a bit. I have heard him confess that, in his early days, he seldom went through the formality of taking a railway ticket to the towns he was intending to honour with his presence, and as he was never burdened with superfluous personal luggage, he frequently managed to dispense with the necessity for unpleasant leave-takings with indulgent hosts and hostesses; and as for admittance to the various race-course enclosures, I am not aware that the clerks of courses supplied him with complimentary tickets, but I am quite certain he never paid for admission.

He was in the habit of leaving his home, bound for a race meeting, with no money at all, or next to none, and every night without fail, whatever sums he had been able to put his "thieving irons" on, much or little, and by whatever means obtained, it was turned into Post-office Orders and despatched home, so that if it should happen that he got caught and "turned up," there was but small chance of recovering anything from this astute practitioner.

38

"They might tear the clothes off my back," I have heard him say, "there was always some benevolent farmer or sympathetic village tradesman ready to rig me out with a better suit. They might duck me in the pond and cudgel me till I was half dead, but I had always the consolation of knowing that the money was safely at home."

It was very amusing to hear him tell, in after years, of the toil and hardships he endured, the cruelties he occasionally suffered at the hands of enraged mobs, and the ingenious tricks he practised to elude the enemy. It was, as a rule, hazardous business to take on Yorkshiremen, and the Captain had a wholesome fear of the Tykes. They were not only keen on the welsher, but when they caught one they were apt to be inconsiderate and brutally vindictive; indeed, they have been known, on more than one or two occasions, to handle them in such a way as to leave them of little service as welshers—or in any other capacity thereafter—and I believe, from what he said, the worthy Captain had himself suffered at the hands of these stubborn and unforgiving Yorkshiremen. However, he ventured to Doncaster on a certain Leger week when so many favourites were beaten every day that he found himself able to remain in the ring all four days, and so successful had be been in finding "flats," he had been able to despatch quite a nice little parcel each night to his excellent wife at the metropolis of the Midlands where she resided. Towards the end of the business, on the Friday he managed to lay a gentleman twenty pound to five against 2 to 1 chance, which was decidedly indiscreet, because it had the effect of making the punter suspicious, so, without the Captain knowing it, he kept his eye on him, and he made up his mind to resist the temptation to see the race, in order to be able to do this till the race was over. But before it was over—in fact, before the horses were at the post—the Captain left his place and leisurely made for the exit gate, having cast a furtive glance on all sides, to be sure none of his clients were within sight. None of them were in sight, so he was considerably surprised when in an instant after the Yorkshireman was at his side, as though he had sprung out of the earth ready armed, like a certain example in mythology.

"What bist t'after !" inquired the Tyke, glaring savagely at him.

"All right, my boy, I'm not going to run away," cheerfully answered the Captain;" come with me if you're frightened."

So the Tyke followed him to a part of the ring which was pretty clear of the crowd. When there, he turned his back on the Yorkshireman, and appeared to be counting his bank. In the meantime, the horses had started, and very soon, unluckily for the welsher, the Tyke's horse won. Whatever sensations of fear or anxiety may have possessed the heart of the gallant Captain at that moment he didn't permit his face to betray, but turning lightly to his companion, he said:

"Look here, my friend, I've had a very bad day, and I find I haven't enough with me to settle with you; but it will be all right, I assure you. Just jump into a cab with me. I've got plenty down at my lodging, and I'll pay you honourably; I'm no welsher, I assure you," and his high military bearing, combined with his gentlemanly and persuasive language, was too much for the poor Tyke. Scarcely daring to doubt, yet feeling slightly uncomfortable, he went off with the Captain, who chartered a hansom, and was soon on the way to his lodgings, He pulled up at a respectable-looking little house near the Turf Tavern. The Tyke was about to pay the cabby and discharge him.

"I'll see to him," says the Captain; "he can wait a few minutes while I have a cup of tea, and you must have one with me while you're here, and then he can drive me with my luggage down to the station." This all looked so straightforward that the Tyke was made much easier in his mind.

"Here, missus," cried the Captain to the good woman of the house, who was in the little back kitchen by herself, "I'm back a bit earlier than I expected, and I've brought a friend with me; get a cup of tea for us, sharp, while I go upstairs and put my things together."

This he proceeded to do, while the good woman busied about the sitting-room, laying the table for her lodger and his friend. Now the cunning Yorkshireman, as he came in, had noticed an entry at the side of the house, and while now relieved of much of the doubt which had before possessed him, he thought he wouldn't throw a chance away, so, as the Captain went upstairs, he slipped out to the cabman.

"Look here, cabby," says he, "an tha sees yon chap come doon t'entry just call me oot of t'house, and I'll pay th' well for it." Then he slipped as quickly into the house again and waited for the Captain to join him at tea, and pay him the twenty-five pounds. The table was laid, the tea was "mashed," the bread and butter ready, a bit of cold meat, the remnant of the Captain's dinner, on the table; but the Captain tarried so long the Tyke became anxious, and the old woman rather alarmed. At last she impatiently hammered the stairs with the haft of her bread-knife, screaming out at the top of her voice:

"Th' tay be ready, sir; thou'lt have it cold!"

There was no response, and no sound of movement in the room above. The Yorkshireman could bear the suspense no longer, so he joined the old lady in the kitchen.

"Hadn't you better go up to his rooms and see what he's after?" said he, a dreadful suspicion coming over him.

The old woman at once acted upon his suggestion, knocking violently at the door; still there was no response. She tried to open the door; it was locked. Then she began to scream. She knew, she said, the gent had been and made away with himself because he'd lost his money at the races. The Tyke had been already more than half disposed to that opinion, and when the cabman assured him he had neither come down the entry or through the window that way, he felt horrified with the certainty of it. What was to be done? They were dumb with the horror and fear of it. A little knot of neighbours had now collected, and someone proposed they should either break open the bedroom door or fetch a policeman who would do it. So cabby was sent in search of an officer, and after a time, having succeeded, the door was burst open, and the Yorkshireman and two or three of the bolder spirits among them followed the policeman into the room, prepared to be still further horrified. They found, however, no indication of a dreadful suicide; no man was in the room—dead or alive. There was a dilapidated old papiermâché portmanteau not worth carrying away, and that was all that remained of the Captain. The active and intelligent officer, after looking up the chimney and under the bed, turned quite savagely upon those about him, demanding to know why he had been fooled in his manner. The door had been locked on the outside, and the key carried away. This was evidently a manoeuvre to gain time while he secured his retreat, worthy the military reputation of my hero. After the officer had made a careful examination of the premises, inside and outside, he began to cross-question the cabby, more than insinuating that he had either allowed himself to go for a little nap or over to the Turf Tavern for a little drink, and so allowed the man to escape. The poor cabby, exasperated at this imputation upon his honour and truthfulness, swore, as only cabbies can swear, declaring he had neither closed an eye nor moved from the spot, so that he couldn't have escaped down the entry. It remained for a sharp lad, instead of an active and intelligent officer, to discover an altogether different and easy means of escape, which was, after all, ridiculously obvious. This was a low wall which formed the boundary of the little yard, over which a person might almost step into a similar little yard, and thence down another entry leading to a street running parallel to ours.

By this means, then, and while the busy housewife had been laying the table for two, had the Captain escaped, and he was on the way to Birmingham hugging himself complacently after another brilliant victory; amusing himself as to what the old woman would say when she found he had taken his departure without the usual formality, and what cabby would charge the Yorkshireman for his exciting job.

The remarkable strategy and resourcefulness of the gallant Captain in this episode clearly qualifies him as a General among welshers; his grasp of the situation, determination, and courage, were characteristic of the man, and worthy a better cause.

On another occasion he was plying his nefarious occupation at the aristocratic little Hunt Meeting, Stratford-on-Avon, but with only indifferent success, and it was on the last race but one when he secured a bite of any value. A couple of formidable-looking countrymen came up while he was offering 3 to 1 on the field for this race; as the straight men were limiting their offers to 6 to 4, the countrymen took the bait, and invested three sovereigns, and then went on the stand to see the race. But they returned before the race was run, and before the Captain had thought it necessary to make tracks. Some unkind acquaintance had put him away by darkly hinting something derogatory to the character of the layer of long odds, so they forsook the pleasure of seeing the race for that of keeping an eye on the man with their money. The Captain saw them and appreciated their motive, and resolved, if possible, to outwit them. The horses had started, and were indeed half-way home, when he walked quietly into the urinal, which was a flimsy, temporary erection—a few boards against the hedge dividing the betting ring from the adjoining field.

The young men kept their eyes fixed on the entrance, which was also the only means—apparently—of exit. While they are watching, the race was over, and their horse had won, and beginning to think their bookmaker a rather unnecessarily long time behind the boards, they entered the place themselves, but the bird had flown. Instead of their bookmaker, they saw the big gap he had made in the hedge as he had torn his way through it. Instantly they resolved to go in pursuit of their money, or revenge. Naturally, they were about to rush across the field towards the highway, supposing the welsher, as green as themselves, would take the nearest way back to Stratford. It was therefore unlucky for the fugitive that at the moment he broke through the hedge an unsympathetic wretch, on the very top of the stand, happened to glance into the field below, so he was able to instruct them in what direction the Captain had gone, which was exactly opposite to that which they were taking. Away they went, having this good scent, as fast as they could run, and when they arrived at the top of the field they were rewarded with a view of their cunning bookie walking leisurely at the side of the hedge in the next field. Almost before the Captain was aware he was pursued they came up with him. The welsher once more grasped the awkward situation; he knew that to run was out of the question, and forcible resistance mere madness; he must needs try once again his oldest and most useful defender, his ever plausible tongue. The enemy came towards him, cudgels in hand and murder in the eye. Under these circumstances, it was difficult for him to secure an opening for his powerful tongue before they opened fire with the cudgels; however, he made the effort.

"Look here, young men," he cried out before they were within striking distance, "if you want to get your money, just hear what I've got to say." They lowered their cudgels for a moment to hear what he'd got to say, and he went on with his speech, with assurance of another victory. "I'm an honest old man" (a good deal of emphasis on the "old man") "and I've met with great misfortunes. I've been betting every day I've had a chance for three weeks, and I've lost every blessed day. I'd only twenty pounds when I came here to-day, and all that went on the first three races. What could I do? A starving wife and family at home. I took your three quid because a fellow told me the favourite couldn't possibly win, and Mr. Wilson himself had told me it was a cert for his; so I put your three nickers on Mr. Wilson's; and now I'm

43

broken-hearted, and haven't a shilling to get home with."

"Oh, that won't do for us," said one of the countrymen, the murder, however, being no longer in his eye; "you must have money about you," and with that they proceeded to run him over. Every pocket was searched, but no coin was found. It didn't occur to them to take his boots off; he had a watch and chain on, and judging they would, most likely, confiscate these, he made a virtue, and something else, of necessity.

"Now I'll tell you what I'll do to show you I mean going straight by you young men. I've got a gold watch here which I wouldn't sell for fifty pounds—not that it's worth more than fourteen or fifteen, but it was a present from my poor old mother who's now in heaven; then the chain is worth six or seven pounds. Now I owe you nine pounds; lend me thirty shillings and make it ten guineas, and I'll hand you over the watch and chain for security—that is, if you'll promise me not to part with it for a week; but let me have it back on sending you the ten guineas."

After more of the Captain's eloquence they were subdued, and advanced him the thirty shillings, and he entrusted them with this precious heirloom of his family on their solemnly reiterating the promise to let him have it back on repayment of the ten guineas. And so they parted, the Captain to the bosom of his virtuous family in Birmingham, and the two countrymen to Stratford, where they lived, and where they soon made the distressing discovery that the watch and chain were excellent samples of Brummagem ware, but not gold; really fairly good imitations of it, and worth altogether perhaps fifteen shillings.

There can be but little doubt that had the daring spirit, clear-sightedness, indomitable energy, and other noble qualities which went to make the bold welsher what he was been exercised in any legitimate business, he would have been a notably successful man. This would appear to have been the opinion of a number of people beside myself, and it was not an uncommon thing to hear the expression of this opinion. One gentleman held it so firmly, he decided to back it by risking a considerable sum of money. This was Mr. William Taylor, who, with his brother George, were well known bookmakers, hailing from the Emerald Isle. These gentlemen were devout Catholics, and were both of them among the most straightforward and benevolent men I ever met with. Will Taylor, being impressed, as I said, with the evident ability of the Captain, determined upon the Quixotic task of his reclamation. The Captain's plausible tongue had almost convinced him that it was only want of means which had prevented him shining in some straight way long, before—indeed, it would appear it had been by the merest chance he hadn't been a saint instead of a welsher.

"Supposing I start you with a small bank to begin with," said Mr. Taylor, " will you promise me to bet fair and go straight ? "

"I should think I would, Mr. Taylor," the Captain replied. "Why, it's the opportunity I've been waiting and longing for all my life."

"Then you shall start to-morrow at Warwick," said the philanthropist. "I'll provide the necessary tools, and be behind you to the extent of a hundred pounds to begin with, and I'll make people acquainted with the fact as far as possible, so you may be able to get a little betting."

With the tears of gratitude welling up in his eyes, and loud in praise of his benefactor, the Captain took his departure; and on the following day behold him in the ring at Warwick, equipped and eager to commence his new career as a legitimate layer, declaring on his honour to Mr. Taylor, and to all whom it might concern, that nothing on earth should make him go crooked again if Mr. Taylor would only stand by him. Well, the first race is over, and the philanthropist, full of excitement, rushes off to see how the new bookie has fared.

"Well, Captain, what have you done?" asked he. But he need scarcely have asked; the Captain's beaming countenance proclaimed the good news, "a skinner" to begin with, which was set down as an augury of good. A clear book for £27 gave him heart to bet even more vigorously on the second race, and he was rewarded by even better results; he had yet another clear book for nearly £40. Again Taylor hurried up to the "joint," and the Captain almost embraced him in his effusive gratitude.

"Oh, what have I been doing all these years?" he exclaimed. " I've been at the wrong game, I can see. Why, if I'd only gone straight long ago, I should have been a rich man now."

Taylor, seeing things going so well, and feeling sincerely anxious to help on the good work as much as possible, now recommended some of his friends who punted in small amounts to do business with him, vouching for his honesty, and even going as far as to have himself a few bets with him. So on the third race his betting had so much increased that another "skinner" resulted in a win of upwards of £60. This made him about a hundred and thirty to the good, and gave rise to visions of rows of nice-looking houses to be called "Straight Villas," with an industrious penciller collecting the rents.

The result of the fourth race, alas! demonstrated the futility of human hopes, and knocked the "baseless fabric" of the Captain's dreams all of a heap, for it produced a low, selfish sort of punter, with no desire, like friend Taylor, for the reclamation of an erring Captain; and this man had the illgrace to put a tenner on the winner, and as it was a large field, although favourite, it started at 3 to 1, so that this inconsiderate punter was entitled to £40 Mr. Taylor, of course, expected there would be a loss on this race, so promptly made for the spot which the Captain had selected as his "pitch." He was rather surprised to find, instead of his gallant friend, one of the punters whom he had guaranteed waiting to draw £40. You may perhaps better imagine than I can describe his feelings when he found the numbers up for the next race, and no Captain. Indeed, the pitch was "to let" for the remainder of the meeting. He had intended returning to Ireland after Warwick, but the conduct of his protege so vexed his philanthropic soul, he remained in England, travelling about from meeting to meeting, for several weeks, in the hope of meeting with the ungrateful welsher. After about a month, he suddenly came across him at another Midland meeting; and so far from trying to avoid him, the gallant Captain put on his high military style, saluting his friend and would-be regenerator with the boldest effrontery.

"You're a nice sort of fellow," began Taylor; " nice sense of honour or gratitude you must have to treat a man as you have treated me. You rascal! You ought to be whipped off the face of the earth."

"Come, come, Mr. Taylor; draw it mild," the Captain replied. " I was really obliged to bolt at Warwick."

"Obliged to bolt! How so? " asked Mr. Taylor.

"They backed the winner," answered the inveterate welsher, looking astonished that any human being should be weak enough to expect him to remain at his post under such circumstances.

46

"How much had you to pay the winner?" asked the philanthropist.

"About sixty pounds," was the reply; " and if I'd paid, I should have had to part with all I'd had the trouble of collecting on that race, and about fifteen pounds of my previous winnings. I couldn't do it—I really couldn't, Mr. Taylor."

"Yes; but didn't I tell you I would be by your side," said that gentleman, " and if you required it, find the money ? "

The irredeemable old scamp sighed deeply, and in quite pathetic tones replied:

"It's no use talking, Mr. Taylor; I tell you I *couldn't* pull it out again. I didn't think it possible I could get sixty pounds back again that afternoon, as there were only two more races; and as the punters had begun finding winners, I thought they might perhaps go on doing it."

The high-principled and generous Irishman, recognising the incorrigible character of the creature upon whom he had wasted his humane efforts, and feeling that nothing he might say or do would have the slightest effect upon him, let him go his way, only registering, mentally, a solemn vow that he would be guilty of no more Quixotic feats of knight-errantry on behalf of fallen humanity in the shape of confirmed old welshers.

For several years after this the Captain continued his welshing career; but he was becoming an old man, and he had lost much of his old dash and daring. And his soul revolted at the brutal methods of the new school of welshers which was just springing into existence. He had invested some money in a commercial undertaking, and that looked like meeting with considerable success; but it didn't go well with his old occupation. But after all, I do believe the factor which most strongly influenced him in his decision to relinquish his nefarious profession was an intense yearning to mingle in good society; to meet on equal footing men of position and respectability, who had been in the habit of looking upon him and his occupation with contempt. To attain this purpose, there was nothing he would not do; he would grovel in the dust, or spend and lose his dearly-loved and hardly-earned money like the veriest " mug." He succeeded in this object, as he did in most of the matters he set his mind upon; but the price he paid for the distinction he coveted was out of all proportion to its value, and will scarcely be believed by those unacquainted with the latter part of his history, and who only remember him as the hard-headed and shrewd old welsher.

Two or three years after the relinquishment of his profession of welsher he reappeared on the field of former glories in the character of a gentleman backer, and so adroitly did he manage matters, he was soon "taken on" by most of the leading pencillers of the ring, and was found betting to a considerable amount of money, with an account every week at the clubs and at Tattersall's. He became possessed of an intense desire to become a member of one of the best and most respectable sporting clubs in the country. At first he failed in this attempt; but with astute management, and after what he called "indomitable *per-sev-ver-ance,*" his numerous efforts were crowned with success. At most of the clubs just at this time, there was a rage for high play at cards, and the game of baccarat was the one most in vogue. The club I have referred to was no exception to the rule, and no sooner had the Captain become a member than he was seized with a mania for baccarat; and night after night, when he was not away racing, he might be found, eager-eyed and earnest, doing battle with the fates at the baize-covered table.

Fate was not kind to him—perhaps it resented his desertion of a profession wherein it had secured for him so much profit and renown—and now, like a very butcher, it had the knife in him. In his own line he never had an equal; at this green baized table he was a child contending with men. Anyway, he lost heavily, and nearly constantly. He couldn't give it up —it had become a mania with him; he almost lived at the club, and the play had got to be a necessary part of his existence. It was known that monkeys had settled on the roofs of all his rows of houses. Trying to recover what he was losing at cards, he began to bet heavier and recklessly at racing, with the inevitable result that there came a Monday when the Captain's racing account was missing, and he found himself obliged to retire from his beloved club in an absolutely stonified condition. Poor old Captain! I saw him many times after that, walking about in complete poverty, reduced to lying in wait for the pals of his better days in order to beg the means for a dinner. He was now too old and broken in spirit to make fresh attempts to raise himself from his dreadful condition. To return to the only mode of life in which he had been successful was out of the question; and if he had attempted

48

it, he would certainly have failed. Welshing had undergone a complete change; its methods would have disgusted the Captain's suave and gentlemanly spirit, and it would have been impossible for him to have mixed with its then turbulent professors; clearly welshing had become an impossibility for him. The friends and acquaintances of his prosperous days, naturally enough, gave him the cold shoulder; indeed, treated him with the contempt which he deserved— deserved for being a fool and not a rogue; not because of a wasted and dishonourable life, full of low lying and thieving; not because of splendid abilities perverted to vilest uses; not even because he owed them anything, or had done them personally any wrong, did they despise him, but simply because he was poor.

It was clear there were no possibilities, no place for him even, in this life, and nothing for him to do but to die. This the poor old wretch did some five years ago. Of course, I am not going to excuse or extenuate the execrable profession of welshing of any kind; but I am bold to reiterate an opinion I have elsewhere pronounced, which is that the Captain, with all his faults, was a gentleman, compared with the vile wretches who succeeded him in the welshing profession, about whom I shall have something to say in my next chapter.

*   *   *

The old-fashioned welshers of whom I have written so far are an extinct race. They were not a credit to the turf, but, as I have said, they were endurable parasites. They fleeced the unwary, and made the young beginner pay his "footing," content to rob their victims and sneak off with the plunder. The *modus operandi* was highly interesting, and, as I have shown, their trickiness and skill in evading the enemy testified to rare natural abilities, and often afforded amusement to those interested as lookers-on. These comparatively innocent old welshers, with their simple methods, were succeeded by what I may style the dark ages of the turf, when welshers "came not in single file" but in whole battalions, terrorising the ring, and setting all lawful authorities at defiance. It would seem as though the good news had been conveyed to the purlieus of thievery in all our great cities that here was a field of labour for the thief, where to ply his occupation in broad daylight, and in sight of the very guardians of the law, without fear of interference;

nay, more than this, where they might be guaranteed the protection of their old enemy, "the copper," if they should have the misfortune to be caught and overpowered by those they were robbing.

Some of my readers, whose experience of the turf does not go back as far as these dark days, will discredit this description of matters, and be inclined to charge me with exaggeration, and worse, though strictly true, and any old racing man who lived through those days with his eyes open will endorse what I say. Many times I have seen these vagabonds caught in the act, and when their victims, seeing legal protectors refuse to help them, rose in their indignation, taking the law into their own hands, and were about to inflict well-merited punishment, the policeman would step in to guard the thief, taking him into custody, only to release him the moment he was perfectly safe. More than this, I have seen the welsher, when pursued, run into the arms of a policeman, demanding his protection, and getting it, too, with the same result.

No wonder, then, that these people greatly increased in numbers, and as they went about in gangs, became powerful, and were indeed a terror not only to backers but to layers also. If a man had been plundered in the most cruel and barefaced manner, the advice generally offered by his experienced friends in the ring was, "You had better put up with it. It's more than one's life is worth to interfere with them."

Welshers were not only thieves, they were composed of the very residuum of thievery. No such blackguards and irredeemable ruffians would ever have been permitted to follow their nefarious occupation, for such a length of time, in any other civilised country under the sun. The brigandage of Italy in its worst times was nothing to it, and if it had been allowed to continue and grow to the present day, it would have put a stop to racing. Indeed, it was only when it menaced the very existence of a noble sport that steps were taken to check it, and all honour is due to the magistrates at Ascot who so construed an Act of Parliament as to warrant them in sending welshers to prison, which aforetime had never been done, thus creating a precedent which many magistrates have since followed, to the purification of the turf in a remarkable degree.

Some of my readers may incline to the opinion that I have overdrawn the picture and am unduly severe on welshers of the period under notice. I answer that exaggeration were almost impossible, and personal experience warrants me—if excuse were necessary—in the use of the strongest language at command. I owe it to the unspeakable brutality and ruffianism of these thieves that I have gone maimed and limping through nearly thirty years of my life, and which I shall do through all that remains of it, knowing no day in all the years, and but few hours, without more or less of pain. It is therefore natural that I should feel bitterly, and say what I feel. At the same time, I know that there are thousands of racing men who would bear witness that I have not spoken a bit too strongly against these cowardy pests of the turf.

I cannot better illustrate their character, and the condition to which the ring was reduced in the early seventies, than by giving "a round, unvarnished tale" of my sufferings at the hands of welshers.

I was betting in the ring at Brighton, in partnership with W. Knee, who is at the present day one of the most widely known starting price merchants in the provinces. I was betting, and my young friend was booking. Up came a man who will be remembered as Big Fisher, one of the most notable scoundrels of the gang then travelling; he took ten pounds to five the favourite, posting with me his fiver. After he had turned away, my partner remarked:

"If this favourite wins, I shall want you to stop a tenner he welshed me of at Worcester."

"That was before you joined me," I answered; "and, of course, has nothing to do with me. But if he wins, and you intend stopping it, you had better take the money, and settle with him when he comes."

As the favourite won, I awaited with some anxiety the return of Fisher, knowing him for one of the most violent and dangerous of all the thieving fraternity. It was not long before he put in an appearance, and my partner handed him his fiver back, which was all he considered due.

"What the does this mean ? " inquired the ruffian.

"It means that I've stopped the tenner you owe me for Worcester," replied my friend.

The welsher, foaming with rage, dashed the money on the ground with a volley of the most fearful oaths, and at once went for my partner, who was then a well-built, powerful young fellow, nearly as heavy as Big Fisher. In an instant a crowd was around them, composed very largely of "the boys," and all was confusion. The combatants were on the ground together, and it was clear that Fisher, unaided, would fare badly; but the thief was not to go unaided, for I distinctly saw one of his pals, a fellow named, or nicknamed, " Butcher," deliberately kick at my friend while they were on the ground. This was a bit more than I could stand, so I rushed in and pulled Butcher away. The fight was, of course, soon over, as the police were near at hand; but I have painful reasons for remembering the diabolical expression of Mr. Butcher's face as he turned away from me, saying:

"Look after yourself, you- -. We'll do you next. We know you're a policeman."

The latter remark, I afterwards learned, referred to my acquaintance with the celebrated Scotland Yard detective, Tanner, with whom they had seen me talk occasionally, although, on no occasion, had they or their doings been the subject of conversation.

Well, I thought the matter had blown over, at any rate for the present, and was just beginning to bet on the following race when a little fellow came hurriedly past me, and, without looking at me, earnestly whispered, " Keep your eyes open, the boys are on you," or words to that effect. I turned to look after this would-be friend, and as I did so I received a fearful blow on the side of the head; in a second I was on the ground, being kicked all over. I was literally surrounded by the ruffians; but I well remember seeing among my assailants Big Fisher, Butcher, and a dreadful thief from Birmingham named Sam Unwin. In two minutes, and before assistance could reach me, I was served fearfully. Among other injuries, my leg was broken in the ankle, and the joint dreadfully dislocated, the muscles being so badly lacerated as to preclude the possibility of ever becoming sound again.

I was carried to my lodgings in the King's Road, suffering excruciating pains, and there I lay for many weeks. In the meantime, articles had appeared anent the subject in various newspapers; a sort of committee, composed of a few well-known members of the ring, took the question up, and warrants were issued for the arrest of such of the miscreants as I was able to identify. They, however, left the country or kept out of the way for a long time, and the following year the matter was allowed to drop. I had all along made up my mind that neither I nor any one individual ought to be singled out for the purpose of prosecuting these villains, not only because I knew the danger to the individual, but I felt it ought to be undertaken by a body representing the whole ring, in the interests of the ring, and of the public. Butcher, from what I afterwards saw of him, no doubt relinquished his disreputable calling; anyway, I never remember to have seen him following it from that time. The other two, after my affair had blown over, continued their thieving career as boldly as ever, and I have known them more than once assisting at scenes as shameful as that described. They were both drunkards as well as thieves. Big Fisher dropped out of sight many years ago, and I should say he had either drunk himself to death or died doing time in one of His Majesty's prisons. The last time I saw Unwin was a few years ago; he was too old and emaciated to get about the country racing; so he was employed on Saturday nights outside a "cag-mag" meat shop in one of the low parts of Birmingham, touting for customers. Soon after this I heard of his dying in abject poverty in one of the slums of that city.

These men were not exceptions, they were fair samples of what welshers had now become, and the treatment I received was not more brutal than scores of respectable men underwent at the hands of these or other members of the fraternity.

At Lichfield, a year or two after my case, I witnessed a scene more horrible than that wherein I was concerned, because the victim was an elderly man, and apparently in a feeble condition. A firm of welshers had established themselves in the ring; the ruffian who acted the part of bookmaker was perched on the top of a high stool. He had hung round his neck, by means of a broad yellow strap, a large satchel, on the front of which was emblazoned, in gold letters, the name of one of the best-known bookmakers. This, by-the-by, was a very common practice, and, in more than one case I have known respectable bookmakers permit their names to be forged in this way, and the public thereby gulled, because they were afraid of the consequences to themselves if they interfered.

Well, the respectable old gentleman I have referred to, it appeared, had deposited two sovereigns with the welsher, taking him twelve pounds to that amount a certain horse which won, and, of course, he demanded of the thief, who had borrowed the straight man's name, the fourteen pounds he was entitled to. In the days of the old-fashioned welsher he would have found the "pitch" to let; not so with the modern type of welsher, he maintained his position with an effrontery bred of constant success; so the old man handed up his ticket.

"How much do you want?" asked the welsher in the business-like manner of the straight man.

"Fourteen pounds, sir," replied the old gentleman.

"Number 725, fourteen pounds," shouted the thief to his fellow-thief, who acted as his clerk, and who, after pretending to look at the book, looked innocently up at his master, remarking:

"The gentleman's put the wrong horse down; he backed a loser," and the welsher tears up the ticket into little bits, and throws them into the old man's face.

"Go away, you damned old scamp," says he; "what are you trying on?"

Some old gentlemen would have gone away terrified at the savage demeanour of this bookmaker, supplemented as it was by the rude and uncomplimentary remarks of a little band of square-headed ruffians by whom he was immediately surrounded. But this old gentleman, with more valour than discretion, was not of that metal. He was an excitable and passionate little man, and he commenced a violent argument, and when he found himself being hustled about by those surrounding him he made a snatch at the satchel, which was the signal for "the boys" to begin their work. In about one minute the poor old man was kicked into unconsciousness, his pockets rifled of watch and money, and I have no doubt that, although no bones were broken, he had received injuries which would trouble him as long as he lived, and probably shorten his life. The welsher and his confederates got clear away to continue the like business elsewhere.

Occasionally these ruffians met with their due; and once they did so, I remember, under amusing circumstances.

A few of my elderly readers will remember the famous Battle of Ewell, which was much talked about at the time.

A gang of welshers, hailing chiefly from Manchester, Nottingham, and Sheffield, and known as "The Forty," were very much in evidence in those days. A party of them, during the Epsom Summer Meeting, had quartered themselves at the pretty little village of Ewell, at whose capital old hostelry some of us have rested many a time for a drink on the way. It is a few miles from the course, and on one of the highways to London, and as in those times vast numbers of those attending the races went by road, it is easy to imagine, if you don't remember, what a busy place the little village was on "the Derby Day." A couple of the pleasant party I have named lodged at a cottage down one of the lanes, and after the labours of the day on the downs, hither they repaired for a good feed and unlimited booze. On the Derby Day in question, after these two young men had so regaled themselves, they strolled into the main road and joined the crowds who were watching the carriage-loads of jovial folk returning from the races. Some will recognise the two men when I tell them they were known as Punch and Iron Mask. Punch was a cobby-built fellow, with a big head on broad shoulders, and a flat nose on a face as big, and about the colour of an old-fashioned copper warming-pan. His pal was a much taller man, with a slight stoop, very long arms, and a cadaverous-looking face, with huge jaws and prominent cheek-bones, which almost obscured his wolfish little eyes. And they were both supposed to be able to scrape a bit; indeed, they were quite a terror to quiet folk, but, as is generally found to be the case with such, they were both at bottom arrant cowards.

They had no sooner taken their stand on the high ground forming the footpath on one side of the road than they proceeded to pelt the carriage people passing by with rotten eggs, sods of turf, and sundry other objectionable missiles, while other of the onlookers contented themselves with blowing peas through a tube, and less objectionable annoyances. Most of the passengers took it all as a matter of course, and bore it as became the day and the occasion. A carriage, drawn by a pair of high-stepping horses, was coming by, and a couple of young swells with two ladies, evidently of the blue blood, were seated in the carriage. Punch and his friend, in an unlucky moment, thinking this was an excellent opportunity for a little extra display, shied a huge sod, which caught one of the ladies on the head, sadly frightening her, and what was worse, utterly spoiled her headgear. This resulted in a surprising deviation from the usual state of things, and instead of the coachman having orders to drive faster, the horses were stopped suddenly, and out jumped the two young swells, and in an instant they were face to face with their ruffianly assailants, and the most remarkable part of the business was that the welshers immediately recognised in the two swells a couple of their victims on the course.

"You two blackguards will have to fight," began the shorter of the swells, " or else you will have to be locked up; now, which is it to be? "

"Hear, hear ! bravo, little 'un ! " shouted some of the bystanders, and it was clear there were enough honest Englishmen present to see fair play, and who, English like, dearly love to see a fight. The welshers blustered a bit to begin with, but seeing no way out of it, threw off their jackets, and prepared for the fray. "You take Mr. Flatnose," said the gentleman who had spoken before, "and I'll have a go at this big thief who welshed me to-day."

The taller of the gentlemen protested against this arrangement, and wanted to slip into the big one, but the little one wouldn't hear of it, and so began the famous battle of Ewell.

As the two fights began at the same moment, it is rather difficult to describe the early stages of them. Punch was a Lancashire man, and believing if he could succeed in getting a grip of his opponent he would be able to trip him up and fall on him, according to the custom of the boys in his country, and surmising at once that he should have no chance in ordinary fighting, immediately he stood before his opponent he made a dash to get hold, but instead of the gentleman he got hold of a blow straight from the shoulder, and delivered on Punch's poor flat nose with a force and precision which not only scored first blood for the gentleman, but made the bully's thick body spin, and his eyes strike fire, ere he flopped on the earth like a lump of lead. When they picked him up he would have run if there had been any use doing so; as it was, he had evidently very soon had enough, and the men who had volunteered to second him had almost to throw him at his terrible enemy. This time his attempt to rush the gentleman was of the feeblest description; he was instantly seized by the scruff of the neck, and the swell held him there till he had sufficiently pummelled him, and then sent him reeling to mother earth. The gentleman was satisfied, and Punch was more than satisfied, and was glad to sneak away without inquiring after the fate of his pal.

Meanwhile, Iron Mask, having an immense advantage in size and the length of his reach, was not doing quite so badly as Punch, and that is all that can be said for him, for, despite the length of his reach, he had never been able to touch his little opponent, who, in point of science and condition, was as far in front of him as was Tom Sayers to an untutored yokel; so he got peppered on nose, and eyes, and high cheek-bones to such a purpose that his wife would never have known him.

It took something longer to bring this result about than Punch's punishment had taken, but it was just as effective, and before they had been at it many minutes Iron Mask knew he had no chance whatever, so instead of coming up to time, after a stinging thump in the ribs, which had nearly knocked the life out of him, he quietly turned his back and was for slinking away after his friend Punch.

"No, you don't go like that," said the gentleman, following him up and taking hold of him. Iron Mask, seeing him at such close quarters, suddenly turned round, a very devil gleaming in his eyes, and letting fly at the gentleman, caught him a nasty blow on the side of the head. This naturally exasperated the swell, so he set about him in earnest. Ding! dong! like little sledge hammers, on ribs, mouth, and nose went the iron fists of the gentleman, till the big welsher was out of puff and utterly cowed, and again would have sought safety in flight. "You don't move from here," said the plucky little swell, dodging round him, but keeping a safe distance, "till you apologise, and say you have had enough; and if you don't do so, I'll set about you again."

Anything was preferable to this, and he proceeded to apologise in the most abject fashion, and declared, I am sure with more truthfulness than he was accustomed to use, that he had had enough, and only then was he allowed to follow his friend to the little cottage down the lane.

The two swells, who had not troubled to remove their coats, and as cool as though nothing had happened, proceeded down the road to where their carriage awaited them, and drove off amid the cheers of the crowd, and so ended the Battle of Ewell. Iron Mask has been dead these many years; but it was only the other day that I came across Punch, within a few yards of one of the principal sporting clubs of London; a poor, shrivelled-up old wretch, ragged and bootless, and hungry, lying in wait for sporting men, whom, he had reason to know, have tender hearts, and stand the "whispering" of the most worthless objects, whose sole claim to charity is their poverty and bitter distress.

Before I have done with Punch, it may be worth while giving a short account of his history, and how he became a welsher, gleaned from material supplied by the redoubtable old welsher himself, the truthfulness of which I have no reason to doubt.

I was walking thoughtfully through the classic precincts of Old Drury. The names of several of the streets I passed had given my thought a certain drift—I was living in the past—the offices of the *L.V.G.*—whither my feet were tending—the wicked autocrat who holds in the hollow of his hand the destinies of all connected with those offices, as well as the wretched myrmidons of his tyranny—editors, printers, and such-like—were all dead and buried, or yet to be born, as far as I was concerned. The pale-faced hungry urchins that fight for the end of my cigar, as they wallow in the mud—the wretched, ragged creature, pressing to her dirty bosom the putty-like face of a tiny child, as she flits past me into the darkness of one of these courts—the blear-eyed thing that was once, perhaps, a man, who reels out of the gin-shop, and rushes after her—all, all, are shadows merely. The only realities are the beautiful women, with spotted cheeks and powdered hair and flowing robes of silk; and the gallant gentlemen to match, all associated in my mind with the names of these streets, and who are thronging the chambers of my imagination.

I was dashed down from this high society, and awoke from these pleasant reveries by a rather determined tug at my coatsleeve. Perhaps it was a second or third sort of knock of the door, as it were—I cannot say, I had been so busy with my thoughts.

"Beg yer pard'n, Mister Old Guv'nor," said a gruff voice. "Yer don't remember me, I reckon—I'm one o' th' old boys." But I did remember him; who that had ever seen that face could forget it? Poor old Punch, whom I had not seen for many years, and whom I thought dead long ago. For a moment I felt inclined to slip a few coppers into his hand and hurry on. I don't want to say anything that would hurt his feelings, as he will probably be reading this account of himself; but in his palmiest days you would never have mistaken him for a member of the aristocracy, a Church of England clergyman, or a Bank of England clerk even. On the contrary, in those days he very much resembled a— no, I won't say what he resembled. I'll only say he looks very much worse now, because, after all, to a bird it does make a world of difference the kind of plumage nature gives him; and I hold with Carlyle that clothes play a much more important part in the world than

58

simple folk believe.

Recognising in him a living type of the real old-fashioned welsher, and perhaps of another sort, too—on second thoughts —I believed it might be advisable to give him silver instead of coppers, and that it might even be worth while to cultivate his acquaintance. I may say that I was never in the secret of his proper name; consequently, I was obliged to address him as " Punch," the name by which he was known on all the racecourses of England for many years, and by means of which hundreds of my readers will readily identify him.

"Why, surely you are old Punch?" I began. "I thought you were dead long ago."

"Well, Guv'nor," he answered, "I've bin welly nigh dead many times lately, an' I've bin awful hard up, times is so different; th' old game's played out, and I'm too old for graft; but I know you won't mind givin' a lift to one of the old 'uns for the sake of old times ? "

I gave the poor old broken-down welsher what appeared to please him, and on leaving him, I said:

"And now I'll tell you how you can earn a bit more. Go home and jot down, if ever so roughly, a few particulars of your own life; how you became one of 'the boys,' with some of the tricks you have played."

"I can do that fust-rate," he responded, quite earnestly. "I'll go home and write it down, and let you have it."

Several weeks passed, and I saw nothing more of him, and I had ceased to expect the fulfilment of his promise. Two months after, however, I found a dirty envelope addressed to me in quite an unfamiliar hand. On turning out the contents, I found a large sheet of a whitey-brown sort of paper, not too clean, covered with writing, done, I should think, with a stumpy blacklead pencil, and in hieroglyphics which taxed all my powers to decipher.

Poor old Punch had done his best to tell me something of his life.

When a young man, it appears he was a mechanic earning good wages in the town of Leeds. He began his racing experiences by having his half-dollar on a gee-gee occasionally at the lists in that town. He was—perhaps unfortunately for him —rather successful, consequently he began to bet in larger amounts, winning at one time as much as a hundred pounds, and so he was induced to glve up his job at the works and follow racing as a profession. The first place he visited with this purpose was Nottingham race-course, and there, no longer relying on his own judgment, but listening instead to tipsters and touts, he began to go wrong. Going on to Stamford, he continued to lose his money, when one of his pals suggested that instead of backing horses he should commence business as a bookmaker. And doubtless he started with the intention of being an honest bookie; but losing all his bank, it is equally certain he very soon became a notorious welsher, as unscrupulous as he was audacious and clever.

The first day he began in this line of business he considered he was very lucky, for he "got thirty pounds and went with it" to London, henceforth to become a denizen of that great city of refuge, which sheltered, and still shelters, many no better than he, who dwell in the gorgeous splendour of the West End, instead of up a filthy court in Drury Lane.

Being now able to come out as a "toff," he must needs try his hand at Goodwood, where he discovered a gold-mine, and worked it to some purpose. There were crowds of simple young swells, like fat geese, waiting to be plucked, and he plucked a good many of them, earning in the four days a very considerable sum of money. He travelled from thence to the gay town of Brighton, where he got introduced to all the old hands at the game, and where he himself in turn got plucked, for they taught him a new game, played with a little box and two square bits of ivory, and known as "hazard." And so he "did in" all his ill-gotten Goodwood earnings, and had to start afresh at Brighton, where he was again very successful at his flat-catching business; getting in his net, among others, the late Lord Stamford for fifty pounds. But, like better men, a mad infatuation drove him to "the box," and again his pals, as he put it, "skind" him.

He then made tracks for his own "North Countrie," and at Richmond and elsewhere made money. At York he met with his first serious check. In attempting to get away, he was collared by his suspicious clients, and had his good intentions frustrated. I have spoken elsewhere of the hard-heartedness of these Tykes, where welshers are concerned, and they seem to have handled poor Punch rather roughly, but it appears there were valiant pals to the rescue. The famous "Stalybridge Infant " was there, and, not liking to see the brutality of the mob, or for some other sufficiently good reason, he was induced to join in the fray, and with such effect that the enemy was scattered, one man receiving a blow which stunned him, the lookers-on believing him dead. This resulted in Punch getting away, but it also resulted in the "Infant" being "run in," and having to appear before the magistrates. Being unable to produce a prosecutor, the police trumped up a charge of attempting to pick pockets. The charge was as untrue as it was clumsy, and fortunately the Infant was able to offer amusing ocular demonstration of the absurdity of the charge. "Look here, your worships," said he, stretching towards the bench his huge arms, with hands at the end of them as large as legs of mutton, "your worships can't believe it would be possible for me to pick pockets with these!" There was roars of laughter. The magistrates evidently did not believe it, for they straightway discharged him, only stipulating that he should remove his leg-o'-mutton hands from the locality.

Punch then went to Doncaster, where he had to be particularly wary, but by the aid of a good "make-up" and a constant change of clothes, he was able to do a good stroke of business, taking down some of what he calls " the tip-top mob."

His next adventures were among the cannie Scots. At Musselburgh he found in the ring a real beautiful " J" in the shape of a half-drunken colonel, to whom he laid an even "pony" against the favourite which won. He immediately slipped out of the ring and changed his clothes, with a white hat instead of a black one, and was back in a few minutes. The Colonel looked at him very hard, and with an evident want of confidence, asked him for a "pony." Punch was, of course, indignant and easily persuaded the Colonel he had made a mistake, but he finished up by generously forgiving him, and then laid him a tenner against another horse which, unfortunately for the welsher, also won. He was now, therefore, unable to go into the ring again.

In the evening he saw the Colonel go into his hotel very drunk, and catching sight at the same time of the notorious old welsher, Johnny Quin, he pointed the Colonel out to him.

"Now, Johnny," says he, "you ready your book with a tenner, losing bet, against that swell, and follow him into the hotel and claim it." Johnny being supplied with the Colonel's name and other particulars, he boldly faced the soldier, and demanded ten pounds, which he declared he had won of him.

"I have not got it down," said the Colonel, "and I forget all about it, but I suppose it's all right; but it's rather funny I keep on paying, and never receive any bets I win."

However, Quin got the tenner off him, and promised to look after the people who were indebted to him.

"You go on to Perth, sir," said Johnny; " I can put you on some good things, and most likely get the money which is owing to you." So to Perth the gallant Colonel went; Punch, keeping in the background, followed him there, as did also the cunning little Quin, and sundry others of the gang, and they didn't lose sight of him until they had plucked him for a large amount.

With varying fortune, for many years Punch continued his disreputable occupation. At times the buffets of the fickle goddess drove him into deep waters, and he met with rough usage at her hands. At other times he made heaps of money, lived on the fat of the land, and dressed like a swell; and there is no doubt what he tells me is perfectly true—if he had saved his earnings like "the Captain," he would now have been a man of fortune, with a charming villa in the suburbs of his native town, a respected member, perhaps a committeeman, of several important clubs, and an honoured pillar of various political associations. Who can tell? I have seen these honourable positions held by men made of no better material than poor old Punch, men who lived for years by his methods—or worse. Punch, like many a better man, has missed his golden opportunities, and they will come to him no more. For him there remains no honourable offices, no charming country villa, but a painful pilgrimage to something quite different.

Welshing is a phase of turf life which has occupied my thoughts a good deal, as it has been a constant subject of my observation. I have elsewhere shown that I have ample reason for disliking the followers of this particular form of thieving; but I have met among them men who are so evidently the victims of adverse circumstances that one finds it impossible to withhold from them some little pity and commiseration. Here and there among them you find smart, well educated fellows who have forfeited good positions and gone wrong through inherent wickedness. On the other hand, many of them were born and reared in an atmosphere of thievery, and so handicapped from the beginning by conditions which made it almost impossible for them to be other than they are. One of the saddest cases of this kind was that of a man I knew almost as soon as I began racing. He possessed, I believe, great natural ability, was quick, clever, and thoughtful, and not having, I should say, a bad heart. Doubless he was as unscrupulous in his methods of getting money as others of his class, and what he got he spent so recklessly, when years and illness came, and he was no longer able to get about the country, he became, like so many of them, a common beggar. When I met him last, which is some years ago, I had a long and interesting conversation with him, and in reply to my question as to what first induced him to take up welshing as a profession, this is what he told me, and I will give it, as well as I possibly can, in his own words:

You have known me a great many years, Old Guv'nor, and must remember when I was a smart young fellow; but didn't know me before I took on the welshing lay. Ah ! that's a long time ago, and yet it don't seem so very long looking back. I'm an old man now, and my life has been a wasted one. I'm nearing the end of a long race—you may call it the Beacon Course. I've passed the distance-post, one of the beaten lot. It's true I had a bad start, and have never been able to make up the lost ground, and it's too late now.

You want to tell how I became a welsher, do you? Well, I don't mind, for it can make no difference to me now. So I'll tell you all about it, fair and square, not trying to make myself look a bit better than I am; and when I've done I'm afraid you'll be saying I ought to be ashamed of myself for an old scamp. Well, perhaps I had; I know I've been very bad—I don't know of anybody quite as bad. But before you begin flinging stones, just you look right into your own heart, because you are better acquainted with that article than anybody else is, and really know, if you would only be candid, how very little you have to boast about. Besides, bad as I am, and as I always have been, don't you go to imagine that I am every bit bad all the way through. If I choose I might call to mind a few things which, maybe, will be put in the other scale; although I fear it will make but a sorry show when the balance comes to be struck.

Well, then, to begin at the beginning, I must tell you I was born, as the saying goes, of poor but dishonest parents. My earliest recollection of life was a dirty marine-store dealer's shop in a great manufacturing town in the North of England, kept by my parents. I could never understand why our shop was called a marine-store. I never saw any sailors there, or, as far as I remembered, anything to do with the sea. It was a dreadfully dirty establishment, this shop of ours, which faced the dirty street. The stock-in-trade consisted of sundry pieces of household furniture, household utensils, which nobody seemed to buy, dilapidated cutlery, worn-out spoons, and broken cruet frames, which here and there showed signs of having once been electro-plated, a few worthless carpenter's tools, boxes containing tarnished brass hooks, rusty nails, old screws, and other familiar objects in brass, wood, and iron, which had been there as long as I could remember. You passed through "the shop," as we called it, into our living room, which was almost as dirty as the shop. Beyond this living room was the mysterious chamber of the establishment; this was what once had been a little scullery. The door which had led into the yard had been bricked up before I could remember, and the shutter of the small window was kept nearly always closed. This was father's sanctum, into which I was forbidden to enter. I nevertheless managed more than once to get a good look over it; I know there was a strong wooden bench with a large vice screwed to it, with files, shears, hammers, and all sorts of tools lying about. There was also a blacksmith's hearth and a pair of large bellows which were worked by a leather strap and a long rod of wood. The fire was kept always burning, and very often my respected parent was locked in the place, working by himself. At such times I could hear him hammering away at metal things or blowing up the fire.

In those early days, being of an inquiring turn of mind, I often got a whacking as a reward for asking inconvenient questions, and for prying into matters which my father said didn't concern me.

As much to get me out of the way as for any other reason, my father sent me to a day-school in connection with the Church of England, and I really got very fond of it, learning to read and write with a rapidity which not only amazed my worthy parents, but surprised my master also, and, I suppose, pleased him too, for he went so far as to have me at his own house two or three nights in the week, along with several other promising boys, where he gave us instruction in higher matters than we were allowed to learn at the school. I was now about fourteen, and it was the happiest part of my whole life; in fact, I may say it was the only part of it where I knew anything at all of happiness. But this good time came to a sudden and very tragic ending, and even at this distance of time, all grimy and black with sin as I am, I cannot look back to those only few happy years of my life without a strange lump rising in my throat, and I can't help thinking that they who brought about my expulsion from that school may have something to answer for.

It came about in this way. There was a great lanky lad among my schoolfellows, about my own age but much taller. He was the son of the grocer in our street, and he and I didn't get on well together. At first I wanted to be friendly with him, so took the liberty of calling at the grocer's shop for Sam Bland to bear me company to school; but the grocer, who was one of the churchwardens, and considered a very religious man, wouldn't allow it, and bundled me off the premises in what I thought a rather cruel manner. The boy, I suppose taking the cue from his father, after that missed no opportunity of annoying me, and he finished up with giving me a nickname which stuck to me as long as I remained in the neighbourhood. He called me "Young Hot Pot." I didn't know the meaning of the expression, so didn't care for it very much, as I called him names in return, which, I daresay, I thought quite as cutting. "Young Sand the Sugar," I remember, was one of them.

At last the quarrel came to a head. We were in the playground, and, as usual, got to high words.

"What do you mean by calling me 'Hot Pot,' you lanky devil ? "I asked, and he immediately retorted:

"Because your father's a thief, as everybody knows, and buys stolen property, and keeps a hot pot always ready to melt it up, and—"

But before he could get any farther with his speech I had landed him one fairly on his mouth, and then, before he could recover himself, another and another on nose, eyes, and all over his face. In fact, I was all over him, and I think he was too much astonished to retaliate till I had knocked all power of retaliation out of him. The boys screamed out, and very soon the master put in an appearance. Poor Bland was picked up bleeding and badly bruised, and taken home, while I was taken by the collar through the schoolroom and locked in a dark cupboard under the stairs, where I lay trembling for more than an hour.

I was dragged out by a couple of the strongest of the pupil teachers.

"Stand forward, Brown," said a severe-looking old gentleman in a white choker and gold-rimmed spectacles, whom I knew for one of the managers of the school and clergyman of the adjoining church. "We have been inquiring into your brutal conduct to young Bland; we have heard all that has to be said about it, and have decided to have you thrashed and expelled the school in disgrace."

I was beginning to say a word in my own defence, for I felt how unfair it was to try a lad in his absence, hearing only what was to be said against him; but they wouldn't hear me. Bland's father stood there, looking as though he would have liked to execute one part of the sentence himself; but this pleasure was denied him. I was seized by two of the teachers, while another belaboured me with a stout cane.

When I got away from them I made for home, and told my mother all that had happened. She consoled me with the assurance that when my father returned I would get some more.

In the evening my father came home, and my mother repeated to him the whole story, and when she came to the "hot pot" part of it there gathered on the face of my father a look I shall never forget. He glared on me like a savage.

"You go upstairs and undress," he hissed out. "I'll give you something to remember."

I knew what this meant, but was obliged to obey. He followed me in a few minutes, and making me undress, he thrashed me with the strap off the big bellows till I was covered with wales and bruises. It was not the first time by many that this sort of thing had happened, for whenever things went wrong he vented his temper upon me. I was a big lad for my age, and, I suppose, tolerably sharp too; and at these times I couldn't help reasoning with myself about the cruelty and unfairness of my parents. But I never dared to reason with them, so I made up my mind I would stand it no longer, but would run away from home and try to get my own living, and I felt sure, if I could only get to London, I should be able to do this. I began to make preparations at once by stealing from the shop odds and ends of metal, and anything else which I thought wouldn't be missed, and which I could readily turn into coin. Mind you, I didn't look upon myself as a thief for this pilfering from my own father, and at that time I didn't think of being a thief. Indeed, I can remember how I lay a-bed for hours at this very time, wide awake, and dreaming of becoming all sorts of good and great things.

However, before I could carry out my plans, something occurred which upset them all, and perhaps changed the whole course of my life. My father and mother and myself had just sat down to supper, when a ringing of the bell, attached to the shop door, told us someone had come in, and almost at the same moment a fellow, whom I knew as Hookey White, came hurriedly into the room.

"I want you, Ned," he said to my father, and the two passed into the workshop, my father bolting the door after them.

They had been there but a few minutes when Hookey was let out again, and without exchanging a word with my mother, he passed quickly through the shop again and into the street.

My father was back in the workshop, with the door bolted again, and I could hear him busy blowing up the fire on the hearth.

I didn't think much of this, because something like it was a common occurrence, but I was alarmed immediately after Hookey had gone, for the bell again rang, and two powerful looking men marched straight through the shop into the sitting room. Before they could prevent her, my mother rushed to the door of the scullery and shouted through the keyhole:

"The D.'s are here, Ned, and want you!"

"Don't you disturb him, Mrs. Brown," said one of the men, "we will see him in there." This, however, was easier said than done, for it was a stout door, and well secured.

They demanded admittance, and my father shouted that he was busy, but would be with them in a few minutes; and we could hear him blowing at the bellows, vigorously, all the time.

Seeing that my father didn't mean to open the door, they threw themselves with all their force against it, trying to burst it open, and they seemed to shake the very house to its foundations; but the door didn't give way. I stood there trembling with fear, while my mother, in a fearful rage, swore at the policemen, and threatened them with the poker.

They managed eventually to burst open the door, when my father asked them quietly what they were making such a fuss about.

"There's been a robbery, and you are suspected of receiving the swag," said one of them, "and we have a warrant to search your house."

"Well, search away," sneered my father, as cool as possible, " and if you find any of the swag here you can run me in."

"You may say that," replied the D., " for I see you have got the pot on, Mr. Brown, and you know we shall not be able to recognise spoons and forks in that."

"There's no spoons or forks there," answered my father, "but only a few old silver watch-cases that I got in the way of business."

While this was going on, a couple more officers in uniform had come in, and kept watch over us while the detectives began the search; hardly had they commenced it when one of them picked up a small brown paper parcel from underneath the bench.

"What's this ?" asked the officer.

"You know better than I do," was the reply; "it don't belong to me." And as they unwrapped the parcel, disclosing two or three silver forks and spoons, he continued passionately: "Oh, this is a plant, I see; I swear you have brought these things with you!" cursing them fearfully all the time. But suddenly fixing his eyes on the articles, he seemed to recognise them, and screamed out: "It's that thief Hookey who has put me away, and you have bribed him to do it !"

And then he sank quietly on a chair and suffered them to put the "darbies" on his wrists. I saw them take him and my mother out of the house, watched them going down the street, amid a gaping and jeering crowd, and then I went back into the room and cried until I fell asleep.

Well, I needn't give you the particulars of all that happened to me at that time, or of my father's trial. My mother came home the following day, but I never saw my father again. He was found guilty, and as he had several convictions against him, he got a "stretch" of fifteen years. But he did not do much of it, for he "pegged out" in eighteen months.

My father and mother all along had been in the habit of taking on a lot of booze, especially my mother, and after my father had gone she seemed to do nothing else. She kept the shop closed, and rarely left the house, or received a visitor; she provided me with plenty to eat and drink, but wouldn't pull out for clothes or pocket-money; but as she allowed me to go where I liked, and do pretty much whatever I wished, I thought it no harm to appropriate the saleable remains of the shop;

and this kept me going for nearly twelve months, and was the means of getting me into some middling company.

My mother didn't seem to care for anything, if I was only at hand when she wanted a fresh supply of gin, and she always appeared to have plenty of money for this purpose. One night, when I was nearly sixteen, I went to bed about eleven o'clock, leaving my mother, more than usually drunk, sitting by the fire. When I came down next morning I found her lying on the hearth dead. In trying to get up she had evidently fallen on the fire and been burnt to death. I rushed from the house and alarmed the neighbours, and, of course, it was not long before the house was full of them, with a doctor and a couple of policemen. Well, they could make nothing more of it than I have told you.

During the day my mother's brother, James Shrimpton— Uncle Jim, as we used to call him—put in an appearance, and seemed to take possession of me and of all my mother's belongings. After the funeral there was a sale, and I went with Uncle Jim to his home, a dirty little hovel up a court in one of the worst slums of the town. I wasn't quite such a kid as he took me for, so I rather put him one on when I asked him, after a day or two, how much money he had found in our house, and what he had received from the sale. I was the more curious about this, perhaps, as I couldn't help seeing that he was now flush of coin, and living very differently to anything I had seen before; besides which, he had never done a day's work since my mother's death. He assured me he had found but little in the house, but this and the proceeds of the sale, after paying all expenses, left fifty pounds in hand.

My uncle had been in the employ of a man who attended races with a stock of stools, betting boxes—or "judies," as we called them, because they were very like the Punch and Judy shows—printed cardboard lists, and all the other things used by the poorer sort of outside betting men. These things the man hired to the bookie, making a pretty good thing of it. During his visits to the races, Uncle Jim had occasionally supplemented his work as an assistant judy-keeper by acting as clerk for some of the bookies, and so had become acquainted with the business. He told me all about this, and proposed that the fifty pounds should be used as a bank to start bookmaking in a small way, and that he should bet and I should clerk for him, sharing the profits, and he painted it in such glowing colours that I readily consented. I liked the idea of travelling about from place to place. All the fun and excitement of such a life—as he painted it—had a great attraction for me.

So it was not long before we had knocked together a little judy of our own, resplendent in bright red baize, and all the paraphernalia of a betting man's "joint." I remember how proud I felt when I saw it put together for the first time on Worcester race-course, and I watched my uncle, with tin tacks, affix our pasteboard sign to the front of it with a swelling breast, for it bore this legend:

"SHRIMPTON AND BROWN:
To Win, and 1, 2, 3.
All In, Run or Not."

I certainly believed I was then on the way to fortune; and, mind you, it was our purpose at the beginning to bet on the square, and pay up. Welshing had never entered into my head; in fact, at that time I did not know the meaning of it.

Well, I and Uncle Jim bet together at that judy on the race-courses all over the country for more than three years, with good and bad fortune. When we won we spent our money freely, so that we never got together much of a bank. We had a good many ups and downs. At first, like new beginners at every game, we had to pay for experience. I remember, nearly the first time we opened the joint, a respectable-looking cove taking odds to a sovereign—which was a big bet for us—and giving a country fiver in payment, and Jim gave him four beautiful good quids in change. The man had backed a wrong 'un, so he didn't turn up after the race; but I don't think he would even if he'd been on the winner, as we discovered afterwards that the note was on a country bank which had been closed for more than twenty years. At another time a fellow came up with a ticket for a winner, and drew a couple of sovereigns. He had scarcely turned away with the money when another came up, claiming the same amount with a ticket bearing that identical number. Of course, we demurred to the payment, but it was useless, for on finding the ticket which we had just torn up, we found that the numbers had been cleverly tampered with, and altered from a losing number to that of a winner. There was no doubt these fellows were working together, but it was equally certain the last comer had the genuine ticket; so we had to pay him £2 also. These and similar experiences sharpened me up a good deal, and perhaps prepared me for the life I was to lead.

As I have said, we never made much progress, and at last we had a very severe run against us. The bank was weak when we arrived on the course at Liverpool for the Grand National week, and there the bad luck continued the first day; favourite after favourite won, and at night the bank was gone; we hadn't a quid left between us. I remember we held a council of war in my bedroom. The question was: Should we retire from the field defeated, or raise the sinews of war by "popping" our watches, rings, and other matters of jewellery?

The latter course was decided on, and we also agreed that we would make this capital spin out till we came to the Grand National, betting little on the smaller races, but taking every shilling we could on the big one, so we should be able to stand our ground; keeping well before the public, gaining its confidence more after every race, and then have a dash against Huntsman, and "go for the gloves"—that is, lay as much as we could against the favourite, which was a very hot one. If we could get him beaten, the bank would again be flourishing; but if he won! Well, we should have to do "a guy," which means get away, and henceforth be known as welshers. Ah, my friend, you are shocked ! but if you will allow me to break in here with a bit of moralising, I would like to ask if anybody knows how many there are among the well-to-do bookies, and backers also, of the present day who have just once in their lives gone for the gloves; I venture to say, if the truth could possibly be known, the world would be considerably shocked as well as surprised. But it has " come off" for these people, and they are for ever more worthy members of society.

So we began to bet on the big race in earnest, pinning our list to the front of the judy, marked with the prices we were prepared to lay against each of the thirteen runners; but as we contrived to have the list showing liberal odds against the favourite, and a little under the odds the other twelve, our betting was naturally almost confined to laying against the favourite, and we did a roaring trade against him. The result was that before the flag fell we had laid the odds to more than a hundred pounds, and had that amount in hand. Nobody seemed to suspect us, consequently we found no difficulty in slipping behind the judy while everybody was intently watching the start for the race. We made for a temporary wooden stand a hundred yards away, where we might watch the race and at the same time keep an eye on our judy.

"The moment we see the favourite beaten," whispered Jim, when we had paid our shilling and climbed toward the top of the stand, "we must rush back to the joint."

"And what if he wins? " I asked, rather dolefully.

"Oh, he won't win," Jim replied; "we have twelve chances against him. Surely one of them will beat him ! "

"But suppose he should happen to win?" I persisted.

"Well, then, we must guy with the swag over to the station, or jump into a cab."

The horses were on the way, and there was no more talk. I shall never forget my sensations as the horses came tearing past us. The first time round one or two came a cropper; how devoutly I prayed that the favourite might be among them. I was fairly shivering with fear and excitement, a cold sweat broke over me; I was actually obliged to hang on to the arm of my pal, for I felt I couldn't stand for the few minutes which was to decide so much for me. In my heart I didn't want to be a welsher, and all the misery and horror of the years which were to follow seemed crowded into those few minutes.

The favourite, as I said, was a horse called Huntsman, and I quickly found he was not among the fallen, for Lamplough, his jockey, had him well in hand; he jumped beautifully, and appeared to be going better than anything, and when the jumping was over and they came into the course, my heart sank, for I could see the favourite still there, and bang in front. As they came to the straight run in the field of horses presented a long straggling tail, with only two of them prominent. For a moment there were excited cries, which revived my hopes and brought the colour to my face.

"Bridegroom wins!" and "Bridegroom! Bridegroom!" was re-echoed on every side; for it was evident young Ben Land was making a tremendous effort, and for a moment it looked like him beating the favourite; but only for a moment. Lamplough called on Huntsman for a final effort, and he answered gamely. As they passed the post—the favourite four lengths in front of Bridegroom, and nothing else within hail of the two—Jim whispered hoarsely: "It's all over; we must guy."

We took a last look at the judy, where already the people were beginning to assemble with the expectation of receiving their winnings; slipping off the stand, we crossed the course and got on to the main road, and jumping into a cab, ordered the driver to take us back to Liverpool as fast as he could go. When there it didn't take us long to pack our traps and get to Lime Street Station, where we got the next train home.

And now you know how I became a welsher. You would like me to tell you some of the strange dodges and adventures of a welsher's life, would you ? Well, well, perhaps I may one of these days, if I can only get rid of this plaguey cough.

It is certainly more than thirty years ago since the true story I am now to relate had its origin. That every particular of my story is true is well known to plenty of people living at the present time, for they knew the circumstances better than myself, and were more intimately acquainted with my principal characters. Four pals belonging to the old welshing school were at "glorious Goodwood" in pursuit of their usual occupation of flat-catching. There were a good many flats about that year, and the merry little band had a rare old time of it, netting among them several hundreds of pounds, living like fighting cocks every day, and getting gloriously drunk every night.

At the end of the Sussex fortnight it became a question what they should do with themselves and the nice bit of "swag" which an unusual amount of luck, and considerable industry, had brought them. Toby Pearson, who was in a chronic condition of drunkenness, although he took nothing stronger than ale, said he knew a nice little pub for sale in Whitechapel, where they did their own brewing, and a good business in ale and porter; and he proposed they should club together and buy it, and so have a home over their heads, and a bit of something certain, when things went a little crooked, as too often they did.

"Pub be d—d!" snarled old Jack Roach; "if we kept a pub we should want only one customer beside ourselves, and that would be a bloke to buy the grains. Let us cut up what we've got, and do what we like with our own. I mean to buy a mangle and things, and start the old woman

73

with a laundry."

"I fancy I see you turning the mangle," sneered Harry Jones. "One thing's certain, the old woman would have to do all the work while you collected the accounts and spent them."

This led to high words, which might, perhaps, have culminated in a fight if it hadn't been for Tom Buckley, who was quite the superior man of the party, and its tacitly acknowledged chief. Those who remember Tom when he was a well known figure in the betting ring and among the outside judy men on the race-courses, especially at the London Suburban Meetings, where at one time he bet as straight as any of them, will not need to be told that he was a fellow with really good parts—with a head on his shoulders which ought to have landed him in a good position. Tom had been sitting quietly listening to his pals' proposals, and thinking all the time of a scheme of his own, and just as Jack Roach was doubling up his leg-o'mutton fist, getting ready to have the first knock on his pal, Tom stepped in between them.

"Don't you be a pair of—fools!" said he. "What are you going to get by fighting? Have a drink, and hear what I've got to propose."

There was an instant clamouring all round to hear what Tom's scheme was; but not until they had had a drink all round, and something like good humour was restored, would he consent to tell them what it was.

"Well, look here, lads," he said at last, "I believe I can put you on a job where we can double the bank, at least, without much trouble or risk; and where we can have a jolly good time of it, too."

"Bravo! bravo! Go it, Tom!" screamed out Toby, in whom the last glass had just produced the noisy state of drunk. "That's the joint for me, my lads, and Tom's the boy to work it."

"You stow your—trap, Toby," interposed Jones, "and let Tom pitch the lay."

"Well, this is what it is, lads," began Tom, who saw that unless he got them quickly interested in his scheme they would be for scrapping again, "there's some racing over in France, at a place called Dieppe, next week; let us work the joint there, and I'll bet we put together a nice parcel. They think over there that all English betting men are clergymen's sons and bankers, and they've never had any crooked betting men there at present; anyway, not any from England."

74

"But we don't know the country," interposed Toby Pearson, "and wouldn't that be rather awkward when we had to 'guy'?"

"I've thought of that, and all the rest of it," Tom replied. "You leave all that to me. Harry knows a bit of French, just enough to shout the odds; Jack can stand by him and wear the satchel, and you, Toby, can do the clerking."

"And what will your 'graft' be? " asked Toby suspiciously.

"Oh, I'll be the 'blue in,'" was the reply.

And as he was the best dressed, most gentlemanly, and cleverest member of the party, they all agreed that he would be the man for that business.

"It will cost something to get us all over there," proceeded Tom, "and perhaps we may 'blue' a bit the first day, because we must go 'straight,' and perhaps that won't cost us anything. The big race is on the second day. We can put up a list on that, and get all the stuff we can. The second day we'll have a carriage and pair posted as handy as possible, and while *mounseers* are watching the big race, we'll just slip quietly off and drive like blazes back to the town and take the first boat back to old England."

The plan was well thought out, and looked feasible enough, and apparently was not very risky. So their few things were soon packed, and the promising quartette were on their way, and brimful of hope respecting the wealth which would accrue from the plunder of the Frenchmen, and each one busy also with schemes for disposing of it when they returned to England.

When they arrived at Dieppe they quartered themselves at a comfortable hotel in a quiet locality. On the night of their arrival they commenced the good time Buckley had promised them enjoying themselves in a right jovial manner, and with such quietude and modesty as usually characterise Englishmen of this class. The worthy host endured with meekness much that he would have objected to from his own countrymen—but then, were they not English *milords*, and running up a pretty bill ?

They drove a showy carriage on to the course the first day, and set up the "joint." And when the racing commenced, Harry Jones, in a horrible jargon he called French, proceeded to bawl out the odds, but somehow the natives didn't bite quite so freely as expected,

75

consequently they did not do as much business as they had fondly hoped; and when they returned to the hotel at night they were somewhat the poorer for their day's work, which was a state of things they were unaccustomed to, and didn't relish.

"Never mind," said Tom consolingly, after a good dinner, "they'll come at us better to-morrow, and we shall make it all right on the big race."

Jack Roach growled and wished himself safely back with the old woman. And Toby, who, not being able to get good English ale, had drunk an inordinate quantity of the wine of the country, which he, nevertheless, styled "wash," was more sour and cantankerous than ever, and it took Tom all his time to preserve the peace. And he daren't get drunk himself, because he knew if he did there would be the dickens to pay, and probably they would all get locked up, and so miss the opportunity he was looking forward to.

The following day, Tom having completed all his arrangements, they went down to the course as before, and as Tom had predicted, the natives took to them more kindly, with the result that before the numbers went up for the principal event they had taken something like a couple of thousand francs on that race; mine host of their hotel having contributed a portion of that amount, as well as introducing a number of his compatriots, who had done likewise. After the numbers were hoisted they did even much better, owing partly, no doubt, to this useful introduction, but even more largely to the fact that they were able to lay better prices than their neighbours.

Well, the big race is being run, and our friends have laid every horse at some price, so it is impossible for them to have *"a skinner"* if they stand their ground, and "a skinner" being what they intend to have on this occasion, they didn't trouble to wait for the result, but while their numerous clients were busy with that purpose, they quietly slipped to where Buckley waited with a carriage and fleet horses, and were very soon back at the hotel. The luggage was brought hurriedly downstairs, packed on the carriage, and when the agitated hostess— who was in charge while her husband was enjoying himself on the race-course— presented the bill, Jones was put up to try to make her understand that it had been all arranged with her husband. She looked perplexed and doubtful but what could she do with four burly Englishmen whom she had heard her husband address as *"milords"*? She let them go, and in good time they and their luggage were on board the steamer, bound for Merrie England. They strutted about the deck smoking big cigars with an air of consequence becoming their nationality, and successful exploits.

Tom Buckley, who was not so bold as his friends, but much cleverer, keeping in the background, is presently alarmed to see a number of gendarmes step upon the deck, looking keenly about them, evidently in search of somebody. He takes in the situation at a glance, and knows who is wanted.

He was alarmed, as I said, but does not "lose his head." The gangway is guarded, and escape thitherward clearly impossible; but with that resourcefulness for which he was remarkable he instantly hit upon a means of escape, which seemed promising, and which actually turned out even better than it seemed.

A poor young mother sat on deck in the midst of her three crying children; with a tiny one at her breast, she could do nothing to pacify the others. Tom, good-hearted fellow, saw in this little domestic scene a possibility of killing two birds with one stone—swiftly seats himself in their midst and begins hugging one of the squalling brats to his fatherly bosom, and thus so effectually blinds the inquisitive eyes of the gendarmes that they overlooked him altogether, while they haul his three friends to the nearest prison, and he goes gaily on to his native land with a fair share of the plunder; and I remember seeing him the following spring going strong and well in Barnard's ring at Epsom, and betting like a leviathan on the Derby.

Meanwhile, the other poor devils had been tried and found guilty, and were then expiating their offence with twelve months' "hard." And this was not all their punishment. They not only had to do the time and the labour, but they were charged a very heavy price for a most scanty prison fare; and, after this, all their money which remained was confiscated, in payment of the fine which was a part of their sentence.

After a time they all got safely back to their own land, and met again on their own happy hunting grounds. Harry Jones never went bookmaking to France again; I never heard whether Tom Pearson saved enough to buy a pub, and I don't believe Jack Roach's "old woman" ever got that mangle; but I do know that Tom Buckley, for years after, was knocking about London and the surburban meetings betting to a good deal of money. But I have neither seen nor heard of either of the quartette for many years, and I presume they have either gone over to the majority, joined the Salvation Army, or become respected members of society, like so many I have known who were, once on a time, no better than they.

I will conclude this chapter with a short story of our old acquaintance, Punch, and then I shall have done with the welshers.

Many years ago Punch had set up his "joint" in the shape of an old-fashioned, humble judy on the race-course at Chester. He weathered the storms of the opening day without finding any necessity to do a shunt, nursing himself rather carefully for the second, which was the Cup day, which, as I have shown, was a very common practice. He made up his mind to go easy through the first two races which preceded that famous race, so he might be the better able to land a coup thereon. But, alas ! Punch was but mortal, and a mortal not blessed with much power in resisting temptation. And when he found in the second race a moderately good field, with one pronounced blazing hot favourite in it, he could not resist the temptation to take the money. It was a case of 6 to 4 on; but by dint of hard work, and accepting a little less than the market price, he found himself with an unusual number of clients, and, when the betting was over, a satchel full of silver, with a liability, if the favourite won, as far above his possibility of meeting as it was beyond his intentions.

The favourite was on the card as running in a bright scarlet jacket, which Punch looked upon as fortunate, that being so easily discernible in the distance. Immediately the flag fell the eager eyes of the welsher were looking out for the scarlet jacket, making ready to move off the moment he had reason to apprehend the slightest danger of it being found in front. No sign of it, however, being there, he boldly held his place, especially as something in yellow was leading by twenty lengths.

The cry of "The favourite wins!" as they passed the post, and a hasty glance assuring him there was no scarlet jacket among the runners, struck him with dismay, the whole truth of the situation flashing through his mind in an instant. He had left it rather late, but he made a determined bolt. Unfortunately for him, some of his clients saw him, and rushed after him with the dreadful cry, " A welsher—a welsher!"

Punch was fleet of foot, and he dodged with amazing rapidity through the mass of human beings, and getting safely through the crowd, reached the street leading up to the city. His enemies, in full cry, were after him. He bolted up a side street, but the pursuit continued, and it was evident some of the pursuers were gaining on him, and worse still, his wind was giving out. As he ran, casting his eyes in every direction for a haven of refuge, he espied a large pair of gates with the small door in them open. Being now almost exhausted, he leaped through this door, slammed it to, and turned the key, which fortunately was in the lock. In a few seconds eight or ten of the leaders of the hunt arrived at the gates, only to find their entrance barred. While some of them held a hurried consultation, others thundered at the gates, and after a little time it was decided to storm the citadel. With this purpose they began to climb on one another's shoulders, when suddenly the doors were thrown wide open by a lad, and a countryman stood there in a "float" loaded with fat pigs ready to drive away.

"What the devil's all this row about? " inquired the driver.

"A welsher ran in here a few minutes ago," answered one of the leaders, "and we mean to find him."

"Well, find him, then," was the surly reply; "he canna' get away from this yard without coming through these gates." Then turning to his lad as he drove quietly out of the yard, he said: "And you, Jack, shut the gates and lock 'em when the gentlemen have gone."

Of course, as my readers will surmise, with the driver and his load of fat pigs the welsher had gone also, neatly covered with straw, and the worthy driver bribed with a promise of a couple of sovereigns if he got him safely out of the city.

The better part of the story, however, remains in the sequel. It didn't take long for a part of the company to search every nook and corner of the premises, while the remainder kept guard at the gates. Of course, the search was unsuccessful, and as there was no possibility of escape otherwise, it occurred to them that the surly driver had done them, and got the welsher away with the pigs; whereupon they seized the boy and swore they would hang him if he didn't tell them all about it, and where the float and pigs were bound for, and they so worked upon the fears of the lad that he made a clean breast of it, and a very few minutes more found as many as possible packed in and on the top of a "fly," tearing through the city in pursuit of that float. Some distance before you reach the confines of Chester at its northern boundary they came up with the object of their pursuit. To jump off the fly and "hold up" the driver of fat pigs was the work of an instant.

"I'll tell you all about it," cried the trembling wretch; " he's under the straw among the pigs."

In another instant the grunters were bundled into the road, also the straw, but there was no sign of Punch.

"Why, dom him," cried the driver, between rage and fear, as white as a ghost, "he's bin an' welshed I as well!"

The fact being that while the man had gone leisurely along with his float and fat pigs, whistling with glee to think what an excellent day's work he had done, Punch had quietly slipped out, behind, and made the best of his way to the railway station; and the baffled backers, appreciating the comical side of the situation, burst into a roar of laughter, the principal subject of regret among them apparently being that they had missed seeing the race for the Cup while they had been chasing a welsher.

*   *   *

Conclusion by R.O.: The first important step towards ridding racing of the baleful influence of the criminal element was taken in 1876, when the Jockey Club stipulated that no race could be worth less than £100 to the winner. That regulation sounded the death knell of West Drayton, Bromley and a number of the other minor tracks on which the worst outbreaks of hooliganism had habitually occurred. Both West Drayton, where prize money ranged from £50 to £80, and Bromley, whose principal inducement to owners was £70 for a selling race, duly took their leave of the fixture list at the end of 1876.

The course at West Drayton, which was no more than a circuit barely in excess of six furlongs, was laid out on the meadows behind the railway station, its owner being a gentleman, who was pleased to style himself Count Bolo. On realising the implication of the impending increase in the value of races, he prudently insured his exceedingly primitive stand for three times its value shortly before the structure disappeared in flames. Being suspicious as to the cause of the conflagration, though unable to prove anything, the insurance company refrained from sending Count Bolo the cheque which he eagerly anticipated. Instead they built him a fine new stand, for which he could have no possible use. Thus two generations of passengers on the Great Western Railway were able to observe Count Bolo's white elephant decline from disrepair to dereliction.

The year after the disappearance of West Drayton and Bromley, Kingsbury also closed. The feature of the final card of the latter course on 20th September, 1877 was the riding double completed by Jack Loates, elder brother, or more probably half-brother, of the future champion jockeys Tommy and Sam Loates, and a third rider in Ben Loates. The principal claim to fame of Jack Loates is that he won the inaugural running of the Middle Park Stakes on The Rake in 1866.

Three years after the Jockey Club had raised prize money, Parliament took a hand in 1879, when a Sabbatarian member for Glasgow by the name of Anderson, who was no friend of racing, successfully introduced legislation. By the terms of the Anderson Act any racecourse within ten miles of Charing Cross had to be licenced by the Magistrates. Alexandra Palace survived, but by 1881 rather less attractive venues, like Streatham, Enfield, Harrow and Lilie Bridge had all lost their fixtures.

The other important element in the elimination of ruffianism from racing was the introduction of the enclosed courses. The first of these Drawing Room Meetings, as they were called, to open was Sandown Park a natural ampitheatre on the site of medieval priory, then in 1878 came nearby Kempton Park once a favourite hunting ground of Queen Elizabeth I. While undesirable individuals could readily be refused admission to these confined premises, they were a great deal more easily policed and regulated than the open courses on which anybody, whether of criminal bent or not, could make a book.

Thus the demise of Big Fisher, Punch, Iron Mask and the rest of the welshers, was brought about by a combination of firm, albeit belated, action by Parliament and the Jockey Club, and natural progress.

*   *   *

Dyke Wilkinson was born in about 1835 in a cottage on Hickenbotham's fields, already a suburb of Birmingham by the end of the century. At the age of twelve he was apprenticed in a factory for eight-and-a-half years, but finding the work uncongenial took very premature leave. For a while he ran a small business manufacturing costume jewellery, before becoming a professional punter, operating, what he, and many others before and after him, have fondly believed to be an infallible system by doubling their stakes on favourites until backing a winner. At the conclusion of the Goodwood meeting of 1864 he was well in funds, and blithely convinced he had discovered the secret of alchemy, the art of turning base metal into gold. At York things went badly wrong, with even the Derby winner Blair Athol failing by a length to give The Miner 7 lbs., after starting 7-4 on for the Great Yorkshire Stakes.

Bitterly disillusioned, Dyke Wilkinson changed sides, and borrowing some meagre working capital from a relative, became a bookmaker. He laid the odds for the first time at Walsall in September 1864. The course at Walsall, which closed in 1871, was on the outskirts of the town.

A YORKSHIRE GAMBLE IN THE DERBY

(Blair Athol's remarkable win in the 1864 Derby)

Introduction by R.O.: The Yorkshire trainer William l'Anson said to his eldest son and namesake, "If I were you, I would not bet, but if you must bet - BET!", some of the most famous advice in the lore of racing. The older l'Anson certainly followed his own advice, as the bookmakers found out when he won the Derby of 1864 with Blair Athol, despite the best endeavours of the more nefarious members of their fraternity.

When William l'Anson senior arrived at the famous Grove Cottage stable at Malton in 1849, he brought with him a number of horses, including the six-year-old broodmare, Queen Mary, who had been given to him after her racing career had been brought to a premature end by injuries sustained in a fall at Chester as a two-year-old. Queen Mary was only a four-year-old when she had her first foal, a brown filly called Haricot, by Lanercost, who had won the inaugural Cambridgeshire in 1839. Haricot, who never grew to more than 15 hands, did not take the eye at all, and as none of the rest of Queen Mary's early foals were any more impressive, William l'Anson sold her for £40 to a Forfarshire farmer.

After being turned out as a two-year-old, Haricot was used by l'Anson as a hack. Supervising work on the Wolds on her one morning, he jumped into a gallop to tell the lads to go faster. As the pace increased, l'Anson, a big man, was amazed to find that Haricot was able to keep up with the other horses.

Putting Haricot into hard training immediately, l'Anson hastened back to Forfarshire in search of her dam. Although horrified to find Queen Mary in foal to a Clydesdale, he was only too happy to buy her back for £100. Four years later, in 1854, she bred Blink Bonny, the mother of Blair Athol.

Haricot, who opened l'Anson's eyes to the potential of Queen Mary, won the Cumberland Plate and other races. On retiring to stud she became the dam of Caller Ou, with whom l'Anson won the St. Leger in 1861. Another of Haricot's daughters was Lady Langden, the dam of the influential stallion Hampton (by Kettledrum), whose male line has been maintained by Vaguely Noble and his sons, such as Exceller, in recent years.

*　　*　　*

Noel Fairfax-Blakeborough tells how the Malton trained Blair Athol brought off a wholesale gamble for the North in the Derby of 1864, although it was nearly foiled by the almost unbelievably fiendish cruelty of a stable lad in the pay of a gang of unscrupulous bookmakers. Blair Athol was a tall, rangy chestnut with a broad blaze, and was known to racegoers as "the bald-faced chestnut".

*　　*　　*

Running for the first time, Blair Athol won the 1864 Derby by an easy two lengths.

Those sixteen words give no hint of the sensational story behind that triumph.

Heroes ... villains ... cruelty ... ingenuity ... intrigue ... and a formidable betting coup that netted today's equivalent of some £6,000,000. All of the vital ingredients of a good thriller combined to make Blair Athol's Epsom triumph one of the most extraordinary races in Turf history.

The heroes were Blair Athol and trainer William l'Anson. William l'Anson had left Gullane in Scotland to train at Malton - which then had 700 acres of wonderful gallops on Langton Wold. He was a brilliant judge of two-year-olds, and extremely astute, but before landing his second Derby, he encountered an unique problem.

Blair Athol was truly heroic in giving him that success, as the colt endured excruciating pain in that most intimate of 'private parts' to win the blue riband on his racecourse debut. William l'Anson had steadfast faith in Blair Athol, but he had to overcome adversity to win - the very thought of which will make every man wince.

Villain number one was the lad in charge of the colt. One crooked groom plus the vulnerability of Blair Athol's 'private parts' almost spelled Derby disaster for l'Anson.

William l'Anson was a stickler for grooming. His stable lads had to spend hours grooming their horses. At a crucial stage in the preparation of Blair Athol for Epsom, a then trusted stable jockey called Withington, tried to make his curry comb into a deadly weapon. Every few minutes he struck the colt's testicles with the metal comb. The blows were administered repeatedly. No wonder Blair Athol went lame. There won't be a male reader who doesn't sympathise.

The other key player was John Jackson, one of the leading bookmakers of the era. Jackson acted the roles of both hero and villain. A Catterick farmer's son, Jackson made his first book with £5 borrowed from a saddler and went on to be a rich man. Nick-named Jock O'Oran, he spent money as though it was fast going out of fashion although he left £40,000 (some £5,000,000) when he died in 1868.

This larger than life character initially tried to dissuade William l'Anson from running Blair Athol in the Derby so that a gigantic St. Leger betting coup could be engineered. But he failed in that deceit, and capitalised on the trainer's confidence. Following Blair Athol's victory John Jackson was the Derby day big winner, winning today's equivalent of some £4,800,000 following Blair Athol's victory.

William l'Anson knew all about Turf trickery long before 1864. In 1857 he won the Derby and the Oaks with Blair Athol's dam, Blink Bonny and here we are have the ingenuity - the trainer had one of the first examples of horse transport specially built in order to take Blink Bonny to Epsom. Before this horses walked and trotted to compete in races - even the Classics. Often the trek would take more than a week. The 'box', drawn by relays of horses, also took Blink Bonny to Doncaster for the St. Leger. But in the Yorkshire classic the filly was 'pulled' by jockey Jack Charlton and finished fourth. She had started 5-4 favourite. The crowd went wild, and a totally innocent William l'Anson - who had backed Blink Bonny heavily - had to be protected by John Jackson's bevy of prize fighter bodyguards. But that is another story ...

Of course, Blair Athol was safely wheeled to Epsom in Blink Bonny's box. We have the detailed account of the colt's pre-race ordeal and scintillating success almost straight from the horse's mouth. My Turf historian father, who died in 1976 - a few days before his 93rd birthday - recorded conversations with William l'Anson, son of the trainer of Blink Bonny and Blair Athol. Father knew William l'Anson well, and was his biographer. l'Anson junior was also a very successful trainer who saddled some 1,500 winners before his retirement in 1912.

Then an eighteen-year-old enthusiast, who lived for racing, William l'Anson junior vividly recalled the formidable network of unscrupulous intrigue and villainy which prefaced Blair Athol's Epsom triumph. There could not be a more reliable witness and these are his words:

"I remember Blair Athol well, and all the exciting incidents that attended his Turf career. The attempts to nobble him, the threatening and almost murderous reception he received in France, his Derby and St. Leger wins, and a great deal which has never been told. In the first place it has frequently been stated - one writer copying another - that John Jackson, the great bookmaker, had so much interest in Blair Athol, or so much influence with my father, that he controlled both him and the horse. This I know to be entirely incorrect. Later when Blair Athol was at stud, the stallion was owned jointly by Jock O'Oran and my father. But before that, though Jackson did make certain advances as to Blair Athol's running, he had no controlling interest in the horse whatever. Blair Athol was owned entirely by my father until Captain Cornish was allowed to have a share in him.

When some foreigners came in search of bloodstock and saw Blair Athol stride away over Langton Wold, they offered 4,000 guineas (£504,000) - but the answer was: 'Thank you but 10,000 guineas wouldn't buy that colt. He's as good as won next year's Derby now.' In fact John Jackson had already offered 7,000 guineas for the horse when he got to know how useful he was, and he did his level best to get my father to sell. I think, however, that my father was a bit suspicious. He loved Blair Athol. He also wanted to have the honour of winning another Derby - and had backed his colt at fairly long odds, and stood to win a fair stake.

Failing to secure Blair Athol, John Jackson came forward with another proposal, which was no more to my father's liking. This was that Blair Athol should not start for the Derby. He, like Blink Bonny, had inherited tooth trouble, and Jackson suggested that the public would accept this explanation for his not running. Jackson had backed both Blair Athol and the Two thousand Guineas winner General Peel to win him £25,000 in the Derby (some £3,000,000) but Hargreaves and Steel - two other big men in the ring argued: 'If Blair Athol doesn't run in the Derby we can all back General Peel, and then get better odds about your colt for the Leger.' Hargreaves, at the time hadn't a penny on our colt and the trio were of one mind: that it would pay them and my father to keep Blair Athol for Doncaster.

My father brushed these mercenary proposals aside. Then came the attempt - temporarily successful - to nobble Blair Athol. The colt was being ridden and looked after by a stable 'lad' called Withington. Suddenly Blair Athol went lame, and was so swollen in that most tender part of his body that eventually he could hardly walk. Of course a veterinary surgeon was called in and with fomentations the swelling went down, and he resumed work. Then the swelling started again. There was at Malton at that time a bookmaker called Rutter. He had come from Australia and he publicly stood in the street to take bets. Rutter came to my father and said, 'Is everything as it should be with Blair Athol? Is the 'lad' who rides and 'does' him completely to be trusted?' My father replied: 'Blair Athol is all right now ... but he hasn't been. I can't explain why he has been lame and I am worried again now. All the more so because I believe everyone here has been backing him for the Derby' Rutter replied: 'Everyone has been - but I've got instructions to lay all I can against him. Doesn't that strike you as remarkable? I thought it only right to come along and give you a hint for what its worth.'

My father thanked Rutter. He watched Blair Athol with still greater care. When the colt again went lame, he made no fuss. He merely said to Withington that it was a pity. But he watched. And he caught the 'lad' tapping the horse repeatedly on a private part with his curry comb as he groomed him.

Father did not wait to ask questions. He threw Withington out of he box into the yard and laid into him with his whip until it was nearly a case of murder. That is the true story"

Blair Athol's Derby was long remembered as one of the most tense in the history of the race. There was trouble at the post - eight false starts. Blair Athol was saddled at Tattenham Corner and led down to the start by Caller Ou - l'Anson's 1861 St. Leger winner.

William l'Anson junior resumes the account:

"Our colt was almost, if not quite, the last of the thirty starters to get away. Jockey Jem Snowden, who excelled at waiting tactics, had orders to 'wait', so the bad start suited him perfectly. At Tattenham Corner Blair Athol was last, but my father kept saying in an undertone 'sit still Jem' ... 'You're all right yet, Jem'. It certainly didn't look so to others. General Peel, now bang in front, seemed set to win. But very quietly Snowden just 'niggled' at Blair Athol and he drew nearer the leaders. A few seconds later Jem again asked 'the question', and again his mount answered and crept closer and closer without apparent effort. Then a voice rang out: 'General Peel's won no Derby. What about Blair Athol?' The reaction was electric. All eyes were transferred to our horse, which was gradually - it seemed almost inch by inch - improving his position. It then became obvious that there was to be a duel between Blair Athol and General Peel for Derby honours. Excitement increased when inside the distance our colt took the lead and won a memorable race with ease. Jem Snowden's judgement had been faultless, and all our worries worthwhile."

There were two particularly happy men: John Jackson had won £40,000 (£4,800,000) and William l'Anson some £15,000 (£1,800,000) The colt had started at 14-1, but many bets were struck at far longer odds.

Blair Athol was immediately packed into his travelling van and sent to France for the Grand Prix de Paris the following Sunday.

William l'Anson junior recalls: "Captain Cornish undertook to accompany him. He assured my father that he could speak French. Possibly he could, but unfortunately the French couldn't understand it. There was a good deal of jealousy - indeed, open hostility to the English horse. As Blair Athol left the paddock he was greeted with a volley of sticks and stones. Jockey Challoner was terrorised by the attitude of the French and daren't have won even if he could. Anyway. Blair Athol was beaten by Vermout with Oaks winner Fille de l'Air unplaced."

Blair Athol ended his career by winning the St. Leger, again beating General Peel. At the close of the Doncaster Classic he was struck by another horse and the injured tendon never healed. John Jackson then bought a two-thirds share in the colt, which stood at his York stud. Blair Athol, by Stockwell - sire of the first three in the 1866 Derby - out of Blink Bonny, certainly had the right credentials at stud.

As a stallion he was a tremendous success. Blair Athol's son Silvio won the Derby and St. Leger in 1877. Indeed, Blair Athol headed the list of winning stallions four times. He was the sire of 474 foals which won 804 races worth £197,438 (some £23,692,560 today). After Blair Athol's death in 1882 the stallion was found to have only half a lung - but obviously that dreadful curry comb ordeal did no lasting damage.

*   *   *

Conclusion by R.O.: But for a strong addiction to the bottle, Blair Athol's regular rider Jem Snowden, would have been one of the greatest jockeys of the second half of the nineteenth century. He used to say that he would give £5,000 to be able to keep away from the drink, but even though his spasmodic efforts met with total failure, William l'Anson and many other Northern trainers used to say that they would rather have Jem drunk than almost any other jockey sober!

Born at Flixton in 1844, he was the son of hawkers, who used to peddle pots, pans and brushes around the fairgrounds of Yorkshire and Lincolnshire. Jem learned his horsemanship riding bareback on the rough, often scarcely broken, ponies that came to the fairs. As well as acquiring dash, daring and a wonderfully strong grip with his knees, he obtained a rare understanding of queer tempered animals, all of which would stand him in good stead on the racecourse.

After being apprenticed to Pickering, Jem quickly established himself as one of the leading jockeys. He was a fine judge of pace, and was absolutely honest. For a time he was attached to James Watson's Richmond stable, and later rode many winners in the colours of the second Earl of Zetland, who loved to listen to his broad Yorkshire accent.

Entering the paddock at York much the worse for drink, he saw that his mount was wearing blinkers. Pointing to the headgear he said to the Middleham trainer Paddy Drislane, "Naay, Naay, tak' it away, tak' it away, a blinnd horse, and a blinnd jockey'll nivver deea!"

On another occasion he went to Chester to ride for the Duke of Westminister, only to find the meeting had taken place the previous week. He never rode for the Duke again. Another bout on the bottle cost him the winning ride on Doncaster in the Derby of 1873, and had he not been extremely drunk he would have won the Cambridgeshire on Bendigo in 1884, instead of being beaten a head by Fred Webb on Florence. After prolonged drinking binges lasting several days, Jem would be full of remorse, and go for long tramps across the Yorkshire Moors in the company of his lifelong friend, Nat Outred. Fit and refreshed again from wholesome exercise, he would go back to Doncaster or York, saying "They can look out for Jem noo."

But it never lasted. His periods of sobriety were as brief as they were infrequent. Flashes of the old brilliance were still seen from time to time, before his obsessional tippling ruined what should have been a great career.

Jem Snowden died in abject poverty at Bentley, near Doncaster, at the age of forty five on 6th February 1889. Paddy Drislane, Harry Hall, another of the Middleham trainers, and Tom Green, who had a stable at Beverley, organised a fund to pay for his funeral, and the erection of a memorial in the Churchyard at Pocklington.

William l'Anson acquired a good deal of property in Malton, including the imposing Highfield training establishment, which he bought in 1863. On his death in 1881, he left Highfield to his eldest son, and the Blink Bonny Stud, also at Malton, to his fourth son Miles, who at various times was clerk of the course at York, Doncaster and Redcar.

When the bookmaker John Jackson became terminally ill in 1868, he disposed of his stock, and, to dissolve his partnership with William l'Anson, Blair Athol was sold for 5,000 guineas to William Blenkiron, who owned Middle Park Stud, the flourishing commercial establishment near Eltham in Kent. The death of William Blenkiron was followed by a dispersal sale. As Blair Athol entered the ring, Mr. Edmund Tattersall asked, "Now gentlemen, what price may I say for the best horse in the world?". A few minutes later he knocked the 1864 Derby winner down to the Cobham Stud for 12,500 guineas. It was the highest price realised at Tattersalls since the foundation of the firm 105 years earlier.

The following year Blair Athol became champion sire. In 1873 he was once more at the top of the list, again in 1875, and for a fourth time in 1877, then through a mixture of sheer greed and utter folly, Blair Athol's fee was raised from 100 to 200 guineas. The leading breeders were disgusted by what they regarded as an unwarrantably large increase, and refused to send mares to Blair Athol. As a result the quality of his stock deteriorated rapidly. By 1879 The Cobham Stud was in serious financial difficulties, and Blair Athol was sold for 4,500 guineas to the Pound Stud at Ripley in Surrey, where his fee was reduced to a mere 50 guineas prior to his death from inflammation of the lungs at the age of twenty one in September 1882.

*   *   *

Noel Fairfax-Blakeborough was born on Christmas Day, 1929. He contributes to *The Yorkshire Post, The Yorkshire Evening Post, The Northern Echo* and various periodicals.

As might be expected from a son of the prolific historian, Major John Fairfax-Blakeborough, CBE, MC, who died at the age of 92 in January 1976, Noel is steeped in the splendid traditions of the Yorkshire Turf.

JAMES MACHELL AND DISTURBANCE

(Captain MacHell's Gamble in the 1873 Grand National)

Introduction by R.O.: Whether the Victorian clerical circles in which his father and eldest brother lived, moved and had their beings, approved of the activities of Captain James Machell is necessarily open to question. Admittedly he was not a highwayman in the tradition of Captain Snow, and other Gentlemen of the Road who adopted that rank, but so far as the bookmakers were concerned, he was little better.

Captain Machell was the most intrepid gambler of his day, although by no means the most scrupulous. While he never broke the Rules of Racing, and would have thought it mere crudity to stop a runner, there were no ends to which that resourceful and sophisticated man would not go to conceal the merits of a horse from the handicapper, the bookmakers and the public.

James Octavius Machell was born at Etton Rectory, near the minster town of Beverley, on 5th December, 1837, the youngest child of the Reverend Robert Machell, vicar of Marton-in-Cleveland. The Machells are an old Westmorland family of yeomen and clergymen whose home was Crackenthorpe Hall, two miles north of Appleby, until it was sold by Launcelot Machell in 1786.

After being educated at Rossall, at Fleetwood in Lancashire, Jim Machell was commissioned into the Fourteenth Regiment of Foot, now the Prince of Wales's Own Regiment of Yorkshire in 1857, and within a few months the unit was posted to The Curragh. Machell quickly obtained recognition as an outstanding athlete and a sprinter, as well as in the high jump and the long jump, and as an accomplished horseman, while supplementing his meagre pay, the only income available to a younger son of a clergyman, by astute betting. One evening in Makin's Hotel in Dublin he won a wager that he could jump onto the mantlepiece from a standstill, turning in mid-air to land with his back to the wall. In 1860 he all but dominated the camp sports. After being triumphant in the track and jumping events on the first day, he won a bet of £300 (£36,000 by 1993 values) to £30 (£3,600) that his horse would take each of the five races for which they were qualified on the second day.

Although Jim Machell was in no position to spend large sums on bloodstock, he did extraordinarily well with the horses which he ran and rode under rules. In July, 1861 he won both heats of a race, for serving officers on full pay at The Curragh, while the following year he won two mile-and-half hurdle races at Bellewstown, together with two four-furlong handicaps, and another over two furlongs further, all at The Curragh, with his useful and versatile mare Grisi. At the end of 1862 at the age of twenty four, the junior officer enjoyed the remarkable distinction of being the leading owner in Ireland on the score of races won, five of his horses having been successful in eighteen races worth £1,035.

Soon after Jim Machell exchanged into the 59th Regiment of Foot in 1863, his military career came to an abrupt end. On requesting leave to go to Doncaster to see the St. Leger, and inspect some horses for Lord Lonsdale, an old family friend from Cumbrian connections, it was peremptorily refused by his new Commanding Officer. Never a man to take kindly to being thwarted, no matter how high the authority involved, Machell sent in his papers, and resigned his commission.

Determined to live on his judgement of racing henceforth, Jim Machell left Ireland, and arrived in Newmarket in late 1863, or early in 1864, with little more than the clothes in which he stood up together with a moderate horse called Bacchus, and two or three others, which were no better. With that unpromising material, Machell established a small stable in the village of Kennett, four miles to the north of Newmarket, far away from the touts who concentrated on the gallops which took place on The Limekilns and the other working grounds surrounding the town.

With the boldness that would always be characteristic of his betting, Machell went for his first coup in one of the most valuable and competitive races run at Newmarket in that Spring of 1864. The event in question was the Prince of Wales's Handicap worth £1,325, more than £100,000 in today's money, run over the Rowley Mile on Monday

94

25th April. As the English racing establishment looked upon Irish horses with a ridiculous, and wholly unjustified disdain, Bacchus got in with a mere 6 stone. Although the twenty three runners included horses owned by the likes of Lord Chesterfield and Lord Stamford, who could afford the best bloodstock in the world, and his unknown rider Tomlinson was pitted against jockeys of the calibre of George Fordham, Harry Custance and Tom Chaloner, Machell bet with cool confidence. By the time he had finished he had averaged 25 - 1 to his money, standing to win £10,000 (£1,200,000) for an outlay of £400 (£48,000), and to the astonishment of everyone but himself, Bacchus won by a neck from Suburban, owned by the Hungarian Nobleman Prince Gustavus Batthyany.

It would be by no means the last time that Captain Machell would capitalise on his knowledge of the value of Irish form, which he had learned to appreciate while at The Curragh camp. With the proceeds from that first touch, he was able to purchase Newmarket's Bedford Cottage Stable, now the quarters of Luca Cumani, and instal George Bloss as his private trainer.

Despite the strong prejudice against both Irish horses and their owners, Captain Machell was soon recognised as one of the cleverest men on the racecourse. His advice was eagerly sought, and in the autumn of 1865 the twenty three year old Lincolnshire Squire, Henry Chaplin, invited him to be his racing manager. Machell agreed and Chaplin's horses were sent to Bedford Cottage. Machell undertook to make their entries, decide upon running plans, and advise their owner when to bet, while George Bloss ran the yard and supervised the routine work.

Among the first batch of yearlings which Henry Chaplin sent to Bedford Cottage, was a small, dark chestnut colt, full of quality, by Newminster, who was given the name of Hermit. After Hermit had established himself as one of the outstanding two-year-olds of 1866, Chaplin, Machell and their friends backed the colt very heavily for the Derby, which was to be the first race of his second season, so he was strong favourite when he came back into strong work at the end of the winter.

Seven days before the Derby, Hermit broke a blood vessel during fast work on the Racecourse Side, and by the evening, he was a very

95

sick horse. The prospects of his being able to show anything resembling his true form seemed too remote to bear contemplation. Worse still, his setback soon became public knowledge, with the result that the stable did not have an opportunity to hedge any of their bets. Henry Chaplin was in despair. He released Harry Custance, on whom he had first claim, to take another ride, and it was only with difficulty that he was dissuaded from scratching Hermit who drifted to 66 - 1 in the betting.

For his part Jim Machell was more sanguine, believing that there was a glimmer of hope left. He stood Hermit in the lightest of rugs to keep the temperature of his blood as low as possible. On the Thursday and again on the Friday before the Derby was to be run, the colt was able to do some gentle work, all of it downhill, and then on the Saturday came the test that mattered. Hermit was given two canters the reverse way of the Rowley Mile - and came back with a clean nose. The Derby, in which the lanky, young jockey Johnny Daley was to replace Custance, could still be won.

The Derby has rarely been run in more unpleasant conditions. After flurries of snow had scurried across the sky earlier in the day, the weather was still bitterly cold as the runners paraded. Hermit looked a picture of misery, with his chestnut coat staring, and his tail tucked between his legs, but to the astonishment of almost everyone, but Jim Machell, he won. Obeying his instructions to the letter, John Daley brought Hermit through with a long, steady run up the straight, and hitting the front a few yards from the post, won by a neck from Marksman.

Having commenced operations with a couple of moderate handicappers and a handful of selling platers in the yard, Jim Machell had transformed Bedford Cottage into a Classic winning stable within less than four years. All the same he was to maintain a close interest in racing under National Hunt Rules, largely because he saw the Grand National as the ideal medium for wagering. Every year the great Aintree race was contested by great big plodders, without even a vestige of a turn of speed, or fast horses with no hope of negotiating the huge fences that were so very much more formidable then than they are today, when even Becher's Brook has been filled. Thus, on one score or the other, a large proportion of the field could be eliminated from the reckoning and Jim Machell knew that if he could find the right article, preferably without anyone knowing he had it, he could bet.

* * *

The following account of Jim Machell's machinations and triumphs with his runners in the Grand National constitutes one of the chapters of *Richard Onslow's* biography *Captain MacHell,* which will be published in March, 1994. The title comes from the appellation accorded to the subject by his enemies, the bookmakers.

* * *

In the opinion of many people, including the Hon. George Lambton, Jim Machell was an even better judge of a steeplechaser than of a yearling. This, one suspects, was on account of his almost uncanny understanding of proportion, which he first turned to good account by winning those bets that he could judge the height of a hat better than the next man during his days as a subaltern in Ireland. The proportions of a yearling change with maturity. Those of a steeplechaser are set and Machell, with his highly developed knowledge of athletes, human and equine, could always recognise the proper proportions of a jumper.

Jim Machell began his association with the Grand National within weeks of his arrival at Newmarket as he ran Leonidas in 1864, when Charlie Boyce had to pull the horse up. Acrobat, his runner in 1865, refused, and after having no runner in the next three years, he had Gardener, a 66/1 outsider, finish third to The Colonel in 1869. Gardener ran again in 1870, finishing sixth to The Colonel, then in 1871 he ran Magnum Bonum. Ridden by Mr. J. M. Richardson, Magnum Bonum failed to finish behind The Lamb.

At the time that Jim Machell enjoyed his greatest success as an owner of steeplechasers, the man who played the most important part of his operations was Maunsell Richardson, the rider of Magnum Bonum.

John Maunsell Richardson was a member of a family which had had property in Lincolnshire since at least the fifteenth century. Almost certainly Machell made his acquaintance through Henry Chaplin, the other Lincolnshire landowner with whom he was closely associated during his early years in Newmarket. A superb natural athlete, known as The Cat, or just Puss, from the feline grace of his movements

97

Maunsell Richardson was nearly ten years younger than Machell, having been born on 12th June 1846 the son of William Richardson, of Limber Magna, Lincolnshire and the former Mary Eliza Maunsell, the only child of Thomas and Catherine Maunsell of Limerick. At Harrow he excelled as a cricketer and hurdler as well as in the long jump and then after going up to Magdalen College, Cambridge, he quickly emerged as one of the most polished amateur steeplechase jockeys of the day.

Having ridden the winner of a steeplechase at Huntingdon while an undergraduate in 1865, and the Fitzwilliam Hunt Cup on his mare Vienna at Peterborough in 1866, The Cat began riding regularly in 1868, and in 1870 won the National Hunt Chase, which was run at Cottenham, near Cambridge that year, on Henry Chaplin's Schiedam. Soon afterwards Richardson was regularly being given mounts by Captain Machell, who quickly came to appreciate that the sympathetic handling with which he inspired confidence in horses, made him a great deal better rider of schooling than most professionals, and that animals, with the benefit of his tuition, rarely fell or made serious mistakes. In the light of that discovery, Captain Machell suggested that he send his steeplechasers to Limber Magna so that Richardson could school and train them, in addition to riding them in races. Cat Richardson agreed to the proposition, although he would accept no more than the cost of their keep. In addition he undertook to buy any potential steeplechasers.

One of the earliest races which Richardson won for Captain Machell was the Scottish Grand National on Keystone at Bogside in 1871. The following year he completed a remarkably shrewd deal on Machell's behalf when he bought three horses - Disturbance, Reugny and Defence - for £1,200 from that wildly eccentric owner, Jimmy Barber, who always affected a swallow-tailed coat of very old fashioned cut and shepherd's plaid trousers, while his long straight hair, which hung lank around his ears and the back his head, was crowned by a badly brushed top hat. Of the horses which Cat Richardson purchased from Barber, he had some first-hand knowledge of the five-year-old Disturbance, as he had ridden that little bay horse by Commotion to win the Corinthian Handicap at the Western Meeting at Ayr in 1871. The French-bred Reugny, once the property of Sporting Joe Aylesford, and therefore known to Machell, and the half-bred Defence also had winning form on the flat.

The first major objective Captain Machell selected for Disturbance was the Grand National of 1873. By reason of his being so small a horse, the bookmakers took the view that he was most unlikely to be able to successfully negotiate the huge Aintree fences and Peach, *Captain MacHell's* commissioner, was able to begin backing him by taking £10,000 to £200 (£1,200,000 to £24,000) By contrast to Disturbance, Henry Chaplin's candidate Rhyshworth was a huge horse, who had been fourth to Pretender in the Derby of 1869. At Aintree he was to be ridden by young Boxall, the son of Chaplin's stud groom at Blankney. On the strength of his size and the high class form he had shown on the flat, Rhyshworth, who had also been to Limber to be schooled by Cat Richardson, was heavily backed by Henry Chaplin and his friends as well as by the public. Also strongly fancied was Footman, who Dick Marsh was to ride for Teddy Weever's stable. Weever was notoriously hard on his horses and three weeks before the National he had tried Footman over four and a-half miles of fences, something that would be quite unthinkable in these times of far gentler training, with a couple of specialist two-milers,who had been winning under 12st. 7lbs. jumping in to bring him along over the last two miles. As Footman had won that trial the stable were convinced he was a certainty for the National, and backed him down to favouritism at 100-15, a little under 7-1. Second favourite was Rhyshworth at 8-1, then came Cinderella, ridden by Jem Mason for the Marquess of Angelsey, at 100-12. By the time Jim Machell's commissioners had finished their work, Disturbance was a 20-1 chance in a field of twenty eight. Machell's other runner Reugny was ridden by Joe Cannon and laid at 33-1.

The weather on Grand National Day, the 27th March, was perfect and the going good. As soon as he mounted Footman, Dick Marsh knew he would not win. The race had been left on the Gloucestershire gallops, and the horse was stale and listless after his ordeal with the two-milers three weeks earlier.

Coming to the flight of hurdles, which constituted the final obstacle in those days, Rhyshworth led with apparently quite enough in hand to beat off any challenge. All the same little Disturbance was making steady progress, Cat Richardson suspecting that if he could only get upsides the giant Rhyshworth he could win, for having schooled him at Limber, he believed the horse to be a quitter. He was right. As Disturbance joined the leader at the last, Rhyshworth's ears went back flat to the crest of his massive neck to proclaim his distaste for a struggle and Disturbance, ears pricked, landed with a slight lead. Leaving Rhyshworth to sulk at leisure, Cat Richardson brought Disturbance away to win in a canter.

As a result of having put his faith in Richardson's schooling, Jim Machell had landed a massive gamble over a horse the bookmakers thought too small to negotiate the towering Aintree fences, which were then much more formidable than they are now. That opening salvo of £10,000 to £200 had been followed by still more substantial investments at shorter prices, and *Captain MacHell* was widely reported to have been a bigger winner over Disturbance than he had been over Hermit in the Derby.

Shortly after the Aintree meeting, Cat Richardson's friends and neighbours in Lincolnshire gave a dinner in his honour at Brigg, where Sir John Astley, then the local Member of Parliament, took the chair. The legend at the top of the menu card bore the legend "Disturbance but no Row".

In those heady days of Disturbance and Keystone, who had won Liverpool's Sefton Chase as well as the Scottish Grand National after being purchased from the Lincolnshire farmer Robert S. Walker, there was complete harmony between Bedford Cottage and Great Limber House.

Jim Machell was always a welcome guest at Limber, where he showed every member of the family the most exquisite courtesy, always opening doors or gates for even the youngest girl, as though she was royalty. Most especially he went out of his way to please Cat Richardson's seventy six year old grandmother, Catherine Maunsell, talking to her at great length about his horses, and his hopes and fears for them. Her Irish origins would have created an immediate affinity between them and she soon came to look upon him with great affection as a totally guileless man, absolutely devoted to his horses and his sport.

Had the people of Newmarket, where Captain Machell inspired a great deal more respect than affection, seen him talking for hours on end about his expectations for his stable to an old lady, they would have been stupefied. So far as the huge majority of the professional element of racing was concerned Captain Machell was a hard and calculating man, who did nothing which was not in his own interests, while prepared to resort to any subterfuge to win a wager or get the better bargain. Yet there was the other side to his character, which he showed to Mrs. Maunsell. Capable of exercising great charm, he could be wonderfully kind and would go to endless trouble to help people, without a trace of ulterior motive. Beneath an austere and apparently unsympathetic exterior, Jim Machell genuinely wanted to be liked, and was rather surprised that he was not. As George Lambton shrewdly observed, he seemed to have two completely different personalities - James Machell, the officer and gentleman and *Captain MacHell* the ruthless, professional gambler.

*   *   *

Conclusion by R.O: Henry Chaplin was the first of a succession of owners to entrust their racing interests to Jim Machell, when they set out to cut a dash on the Turf on receiving their inheritances. Others amongst Captain Machell's Young Men, as they were known on the course, were the Yorkshire baronet Sir Charles Legard, the Seventh Earl of Aylesford, the second Lord Gerard and the banking heir, Harry McCalmont. Inevitably, some, like Lord Rodney, ruined themselves by reckless betting. Jim Machell was widely blamed for their downfall and was accused of encouraging them in their folly That was most unfair. Had the likes of Lord Rodney confined themselves to backing the fancied runners from Bedford Cottage, instead of punting heavily on other peoples' horses, hard though Machell tried to dissuade them from doing so, they would not have dissipated their fortunes. They lost their money by ignoring Machell's advice, not by taking it.

The racing career of Henry Chaplin, a large heavy man, with a thick thatch of chestnut hair and a monocle, was hardly less disastrous than that of Lord Rodney. Less than two years after winning the Derby with Hermit, whom he retired to stud at Blankney, his magnificent Lincolnshire estate, Chaplin was obliged to sell the remaining twenty moderation, with horses in various stables, other than Bedford Cottage, until his final runner, Yesteryear, carried his colours successfully at Chester in 1897.

In due course, Chaplin, a splendid spendthrift, had no option but to sell Blankney at the behest of his creditors, and become a virtual pensioner of his brother-in-law, the Duke of Sutherland. For thirty years he had an apartment in Stafford House, the Duke's London residence, now the Stafford Hotel off Jermyn Street.

Happily, self-induced indigence did not deprive Henry Chaplin of a glittering political career. He was a Member of Parliament for many years, being in the Cabinet as President of the Board of Agriculture from 1889 until 1892, and eventually being raised to the peerage as Viscount Chaplin in 1916.

Long before the First World War had come to an end in 1918, this archetypal, albeit landless, Victorian squire had become an anachronism, to whom almost every aspect of modern life was anathema. He died at the age of eighty two in 1923, full of honours, but with a net personalty of nil.

After losing interest in the Grand National, Jim Machell continued to enjoy enormous success with the horses under his management in the Bedford Cottage stable. He was associated with a second Derby winner when Sir John Willoughby's Harvester ran a dead heat at Epsom in 1884, and a third as a result of Isinglass carrying the colours of Harry McCalmot successfully in 1893. Shortly after Isinglass had completed the Triple Crown in the St. Leger, Jim Machell was taken seriously ill while staying at The Adelphi, Liverpool, during the Aintree Autumn meeting, and spent the winter in Algiers in an attempt to regain good health.

He never really recovered, and in order to reduce his commitments sold Bedford Cottage to Harry McCalmont, while installing his former jockey George Chaloner in Newmarket's Chetwynd House Stable, now known as Machell Place, to train the few horses in which he retained an interest. The closing years of the life of Jim Machell were spent in almost unremitting agony due to a stone in his kidney. Long spells away from Newmarket in the milder climate of the continental resorts, and the bracing seaside atmosphere of Hastings brought very little respite.

and the bracing seaside atmosphere of Hastings brought very little respite.

The last of the 540 winners of more than £110,000 (over £8,000,000) that he owned was Lady Help, whom Danny Maher rode to beat Wolfshall by four lengths at Lincoln on 18th March 1902. Less than two months later James Octavius Machell one of the cleverest betting men ever known on the English Turf, died at Hastings on 11th May.

*   *   *

Richard Onslow was born near Guildford in Surrey, in 1933, and was educated at Monkton Combe School, Bath. He joined the staff of *The Sporting Chronicle* in Manchester in 1954, and was resident correspondent at Newmarket in 1955, before becoming a feature writer, until joining the London Office of Thomson Regional Newspapers, as racing correspondent in 1966. Since 1983 he has been a freelance, contibuting to *The Sporting Life, Horse and Hound, The Field* and *Raceform,* as well as *The Daily Telegraph, The Times* and other National newspapers. He has also contributed entries to *The Dictionary of National Biography.*

He is the author of *The Squire,* a biography of 'Abington' Baird, published by Harrap in 1980, *Headquarters, A History of Newmarket and Its Racing* (Great Ouse Press, 1983) and *Royal Ascot* (Crowood Press, 1990), while he has collaborated in the writing of a number of other books, including *The Biographical Encyclopaedia of British Flat Racing* (Macdonald and Jane's 1978), with Roger Mortimer and Peter Willett.

Since 1976, he and his wife have lived at Windlesham, in Surrey, four miles from Ascot. They have one daughter.

A DERBY SACRIFICED FOR A CAMBRIDGESHIRE

(The Gretton Gamble of 1878)

Introduction by R.O.: For more than two hundred years Royalty and Rajahs, American millionaires and Arab potentates, peers and tycoons, together with a wide variety of criminals, have gone to endless lengths and extraordinary expense in their attempts to win the Derby. Most have met with abject failure. All the same Frederick Gretton, the brewer of Bass, Ratcliffe and Gretton fame, passed over an outstanding chance of success in the Derby of 1878 by keeping his high class colt Isonomy on ice for a massive gamble in the Cambridgeshire.

Isonomy was a bay colt by Sterling, a temperamental, rather vicious, horse, whom Mr Gretton leased during the latter part of his racing career. As well as being an inordinately heavy gambler, Fred Gretton was more than mildly eccentric, with a strong streak of romanticism, so that as well as relishing the prospect of a very heavy punt on Isonomy in the Cambridgeshire, he was more than a little attracted by the idea of seeing the colt avenging his sire in Newmarket's great autumn handicap.

Having been runner-up to Bothwell in the Two Thousand Guineas in 1871, Sterling carried top weight of 9 st. 7 lbs. in the Cambridgeshire of 1873, with George Fordham booked to ride by the trainer Roughton, formerly head lad to Tom Taylor at Manton. Fordham had already been champion jockey fourteen times, and was still only 36 years of age, but was fast losing his nerve, largely due to liberality of libation. On going to ride work on the mercurial Sterling, he was horrified to see the colt bucking and lashing out ferociously as the lad rode him up to the gallops along with the rest of the string and thereupon diffidently declined to take the mount on the colt in the Cambridgeshire, telling Roughton he feared that he was no longer strong enough to handle such a horse. Asked by the exasperated Roughton who should be engaged for Sterling, Fordham recommended his cricketing, rat-catching friend Harry Custance.

That Cambridgeshire of 1873 was run on a bitterly cold day, when a perpetual downpour compounded the discomfort of everybody exposed to the elements on Newmarket Heath. Quite the strongest, and one of the most intelligent jockeys of the mid-Victorian era, Harry Custance had been put on the odds of £1,000 to nothing by Gretton, desperate to find the right man for Sterling on the defection of the incipient alcoholic Fordham, but in those climatic conditions, Custance found he had no chance of riding the race he had wanted to do.

In his highly readable memoirs *Riding Recollections and Turf Stories* (Edward Arnold, 1894), Harry Custance wrote "It was an unlucky day for me when I rode him (Sterling) in the Cambridgeshire. It rained torrents, and was dreadfully cold; I had been wasting for other races, and we were about three-quarters of an hour at the post. There were 37 runners and Sterling, who had behaved himself pretty well in the first ten minutes, became almost unmanageable afterwards. He reared, kicked, and did everything he should not have done as his temper was upset. At last the flag fell to a straggling start, and before we had gone 200 yards I was in the first three, with 9 st. 7 lbs. on, when we had gone a quarter of a mile I was second, with my reins like soft soap. I ought really have been 19th or 20th with top weight on, but it could not be helped, as I was perfectly helpless; my hands were numbed, and the sweat from the horse's neck made the reins quite past holding - in fact I was under every possible disadvantage, although I finished third."

Fred Gretton resolved to back Isonomy to avenge that honourable defeat in the Cambridgeshire on the part of his sire.

* * *

John Porter was responsible for two volumes of autobiography. The first, simply entitled *Kingsclere*, was written in the third person in collaboration with Byron Webber, and published by Chatto & Windus in 1896. The second, *John Porter of Kingsclere*, was written in the first person, with the assistance of Edward Moorhouse, and came from Grant Richards in 1919, fourteen years after the author's retirement, publication having been delayed by the outbreak of war in 1914. This account of the racing career of Isonomy comes from the second book.

*   *   *

In the summer of 1876 I went to the Yardley Stud, near Birmingham, to see the yearlings the Grahams were sending to Doncaster to be sold. During my tour of the paddocks I was accompanied by the two brothers, George and Young, and also by their sister, Miss Graham, who took an active part in the management of the stud. She was, as usual, wearing a short skirt and leggings. The two brothers were corn merchants in Birmingham, and acted as agents for Messrs. Bass in the purchase of barley in their locality. I saw about twenty yearlings in one paddock we entered, and after looking them over, was particularly impressed by the smallest of them all, a bay colt by Sterling out of Isola Bella. His size was partly accounted for by his being a May foal. And here let me state that I have never known or heard of a May foal that became a roarer.

The Grahams made the colts gallop round the paddock by rattling sticks in their hats, and I noticed the little fellow to whom I had taken a fancy threading his way through the others as if determined to get to the front. There and then I made up my mind I would buy him at Doncaster. While we were returning to Birmingham the question of a suitable name for the youngster was discussed. When we reached the Grahams' house a dictionary was consulted. In it we found the name Isonomy, which means "an equal distribution of rights and privileges." That, we thought, exactly fitted the colt, for he had given us the impression that, small though he was, he felt he was quite equal to the others and entitled to the same respect.

In due course Isonomy went to Doncaster and was bought on behalf of Mr. Gretton for 360 guineas. He was always on the small side; while in training he did not measure more than 15.2. He, however, gave one the impression he considered himself a deal bigger than he was. Resolution and grit were conspicuous traits in his character, and he had a very hardy constitution.

We did not race Isonomy until August of the following year, his first outing being in the Brighton Club Two-year-old Stakes, for which he started second favourite. He was a poor third. At Newmarket, in October, ridden by Charles Wood, he won a Nursery over the last half of the Rowley Mile, and a month later was beaten a head in a similar race over the same course. It has often been said that it is a pity Isonomy was not given the chance of winning the Derby. He was entered both for that event and the St. Leger, but Mr. Gretton decided to keep him off the racecourse till the autumn of that year.

The Cambridgeshire was, in fact, Isonomy's only race as a three-year-old. If I remember rightly, Mr. Gretton's policy was dictated by the idea that it was wisest to allow the colt to take matters easily so that he might have every possible chance to grow and develop. Though the Cambridgeshire was not run until the Houghton Meeting at the end of October, we took Isonomy to Newmarket along with the horses we were racing at the first October gathering, a month earlier. At the Second October Meeting Mr. Gretton's colt Antient Pistol, receiving 2 lb. for a year, ran a dead-heat in a welter handicap over the Ditch Mile with Count Festetics' Aventurier. He had won three other races earlier in the season. A day or two after the dead-heat had been run we tried Isonomy as follows:

Cambridgeshire Course

Antient Pistol, 3 yrs., 6 st. 7 lb.		Graves 1
Isonomy, 3 yrs., 8 st. 5 lb.		Fordham 2
Harbinger, 4 yrs., 8 st. 9 lb.		T. Cannon 3
Singleton, 3 yrs., 7 st.		Huxtable 4

Won by a neck; six lengths between second and third; two lengths between third and fourth.

Harbinger, in June, won a mile race at Manchester; the week of the trial he started second favourite for the Cesarewitch, carrying 7 st., but was unplaced. Singleton was a winner of four races that season prior to the trial. The "tackle," therefore, was fairly good, but unfortunately the test was almost abortive. Mr. Gretton and I drove to the stand on the Rowley Mile to see the jockeys weighed out, and on our way thither kept our eyes on the trial ground to see that all was clear. Everything being in readiness, we drove back to the Portland Stand (no longer in existence), where the gallop was to finish. Before reaching our "observation post" we found, to our dismay, that while we were down at the Rowley Mile Stand two rows of "dolls" had been placed across

108

the course. We stopped the trap, ran across the Heath, and just had time to remove the centre "dolls" in the lower row before our horses raced up. The jockeys had, as it happened, seen the barriers in their path, and were already easing their horses, so no harm resulted, except that we were left in a state of perplexity concerning the merits of Isonomy.

Several people saw the trial, and it was quickly noised abroad that Isonomy had been beaten. The public, therefore, had no inducement to back him. Mr. Gretton, who betted pretty freely, already stood to win £40,000 (£4,800,000) on his horse. If the trial had not been interfered with he would doubtless have increased his commitments; in the circumstances he decided to let matters stand as they were. Isonomy carried 7 st. 1 lb. in the Cambridgeshire, started with odds of 40 to 1 laid against him, and won easily by two lengths from Lord Rosebery's Touchet, with the latter's stable companion, Robert Peck's La Merveille, third, only a head behind. Lord Ellesmere's Hampton, 9 st. 3 lb., finished fourth. There were thirty eight runners in that Cambridgeshire, and so readily did Isonomy beat this huge field that I firmly believe he could have carried 9 st. and still have won.

We were now reaping the fruit resulting from the patient policy pursued with Isonomy.

Though he had not grown in height, he had acquired strength, and with it increased racing ability. My experience convinces me that a vast number of horses are ruined by being unduly forced as two-year-olds, and sometimes as three-year-olds. It is foolish to imagine that because some horses take no harm when frequently raced while their powers are maturing, others can, with impunity, be treated in the same way. Every horse is a law unto himself. His characteristics must be carefully studied, and the trainer, having made up his mind as to the best course to pursue, fails in his duty if he does not advise the owner to act in accordance with his conclusions. The temptation to exploit a two-year-old for the mere sake of obtaining a quick return is a baneful one, and more often than not owners who give way to it are blameworthy.

Isonomy, as a four-year-old, won six of the eight races in which he ran. His record that season began and ended with a defeat. In the Newmarket Handicap, at the Craven Meeting, he failed by a length and a half to give two years and 8 lb. to Mr. Lorillard's Parole over the last twelve furlongs of the Beacon Course; in the Cesarewitch, handicapped at 9 st. 10 lb., he was badly bumped by our own horse Westbourne, in the Dip, a furlong from home. But for this interference he would almost certainly have finished first or second.

The defeat of Isonomy in the Newmarket Handicap caused quite a sensation; perhaps it would be more correct to say the victory of Parole did. The winner, owned by the American tobacco magnate Mr. P. Lorillard, had come across the Atlantic the previous autumn, bringing with him something of a reputation. A gelding by Leamington out of a Lexington mare, he was six years old when he met Isonomy. It was his first race in England. Isonomy was giving Parole two years and 8 lb., but started favourite at 7 to 4. Against the American horse odds of 100 to 15 were laid. The latter was said to have been well tried "against the clock" in the approved Yankee fashion, and he beat Isonomy a length and a half. The public at once jumped to the conclusion that Parole would win the City and Suburban the following week, for, including a 5 lb. penalty, his weight was only 8 st. 7 lb.. And the public were right; Parole not only won the City and Suburban, but also the Great Metropolitan with a 10 lb. penalty. So great a certainty was he for the latter that only one horse opposed him. Shortly afterwards Parole started an odds-on favourite for the Chester Cup, but in that race was fourth only. After the Newmarket Handicap there was some talk of Isonomy and Parole being matched to run a mile and a half at level weights for £5,000 (£600,000) but nothing came of the suggestion.

With regard to the Cesarewitch, Mr. Gretton, I believe, backed Westbourne to win only and Isonomy merely to get a "place." It was said that he stood to clear £50,000 (£6,000,000) over Westbourne. When Isonomy received the bump from Westbourne which nearly knocked him over, he was making a splendid effort to catch Chippendale, who had taken up the running at the Bushes, two furlongs from home. Chippendale won by a length and a half from Westbourne, and it is my firm belief that, with a clear run, Isonomy would have beaten him. Our two horses were running on their merits. Westbourne was third favourite at 100 to 15 but backers of Isonomy got 66 to 1.

After the Cesarewitch, Westbourne at once became a public fancy for the Cambridgeshire. He was, however, scratched because Mr. Gretton could not get what he considered fair odds to the money he wished to put on. This action caused a rare hubbub. Mr. Gretton retaliated by stating that he would win the Cambridgeshire with Harbinger, a five-year-old by Pero Gomez. We also had the three-year-old Falmouth in the race. As a matter of fact, Harbinger was no longer at Kingsclere; he had gone to his owner's place and was being looked after by a groom. In the circumstances the public laughed at Mr. Gretton's brag, and backed Falmouth, who had started at 14 to 1 for the Derby that year, and not run since. While under my care Harbinger had shown some pretty good form. As a three-year-old he won the Brighton Stakes and a handicap at Lewes, and ran second both for the Esher Stakes at Sandown Park and the Chesterfield Cup at Goodwood. The next year he won the De Trafford Cup at Manchester. In the season with which we are now dealing, he started favourite for the Manchester Cup and finished fourth, ran second in the Salford Borough Handicap, third in the Royal Hunt Cup, and second in the Ascot Plate. He actually ran in the Cambridgeshire, but was a forlorn outsider, whereas Falmouth was the third favourite. They were both unplaced.

Between the two defeats with which we have been dealing Isonomy won the following six races:

THE GOLD VASE (2 miles) at Ascot, beating Silvio (giving 7 lb.) half a length.

THE GOLD CUP (2½ miles) at Ascot, beating Insulaire two lengths, with Touchet, Jannette, Exmouth, and Verneuil behind .

THE GOODWOOD CUP (2½ miles), beating The Bear three lengths, with Parole (received 12 lb.), Touchet (received 3 lb.), and two others behind.

THE BRIGHTON CUP (2 miles), beating three opponents.

THE GREAT EBOR HANDICAP (2 miles), carrying 9 st. 8 lb. (including a 5 lb. penalty) and giving from 31 lb. to 56 lb. to his four opponents, and with 11 to 8 betted on him. This was a great performance, a portion of the course being under water and the going terribly heavy.

THE DONCASTER CUP (2 miles 5 furlongs), beating Jannette by a head, with two others a long way behind.

This was a splendid record, one which fully explains the exalted estimate of Isonomy's merits taken by the compiler of the Cesarewitch Handicap. A word may be added with regard to the Brighton Cup. Mr. Gretton had a horse called Monk entered, as well as Isonomy. Monk was sent to make running for his stable companion. The conditions of the race stipulated that four horses, *belonging to different owners,* must compete. As the time for the contest drew near we discovered that, in addition to our two, the only arrivals were Sir John Astley's Drumhead and Tom Jennings's Paul Cray. The difficulty thus created was solved by Mr. Gretton selling Monk to me for £200, and he ran in my name. I did very well with the horse. That year he won me three races worth £454 and another of £102 in 1880, when I sold him. He was the first winner to carry my colours— "cherry, black belt and cap" —a variant of those registered by Sir Joseph Hawley. In 1877 Monk, then a three-year-old, started second favourite for the Stewards' Cup at Goodwood. We tried him a few days previously, and he just failed to do what we asked of him. The gallop finished on some rising ground, and Mr. Gretton, who was present, concluded that this was the hindrance to Monk. "The easy course at Goodwood will just suit him," he said. I, however, assured him I generally found the form shown in our home trials worked out correctly. It did so in this case. Monk had won the Stewards' Cup at the end of five furlongs, but Sir W. Throckmorton's Herald beat him at the finish.

As a five-year-old, in 1880 Isonomy rounded off his career on the Turf by winning the Manchester Cup and the Ascot Cup, the only races he ran that season. The Manchester Cup was a handicap of £2,000 (£240,000) decided over a mile and five furlongs, and Isonomy was called upon to carry the enormous burden of 9 st. 12 lb., a weight which is easily a "record" for that event. Ridden by Tom Cannon, he beat, by a neck, Mr. R. C. Naylor's three-year-old The Abbot, to whom he gave 45 lb. The public's estimate of Isonomy's chance may be gauged from the fact that odds of 16 to 1 were laid against him. When he passed the post at the head of the field, winners and losers united in raising a great volume of cheers, and seldom, surely, has a horse been more deserving of the plaudits of a racecourse crowd. It was a magnificent achievement.

Mr. Gretton was a big winner over Isonomy that day, but he nearly lost his trainer. The day before the race he asked me to inform Tom Cannon that he was "on" £1,000 (£120,000) to nothing

No hint was given that I was to receive anything. Although I had saddled many good winners for Mr. Gretton I had received nothing from him not even a "thank you." Apparently I was once more to be left unrewarded, and I felt very upset by this indifference to my services. After turning things over in my mind, I went to Mr. Gretton's factotum, John Princep, and told him of Tom Cannon's prospective reward. Then I added, "You can tell Mr. Gretton that if I am not treated the same as Tom Cannon he can take his horses away from Kingsclere on Monday. I am sick of seeing the jockey get everything and the trainer nothing." When the race was over, and having heard nothing, I saw Princep again and told him I was going to call on Mr. Gretton at his hotel the following morning. I duly called at the hotel, to find Mr. Gretton still in bed. I therefore went upstairs and knocked smartly on his door. "Come in," said Mr. Gretton. As I entered, he swung his legs off the bed, and before I had time to utter a word he exclaimed, "Mind, you are on the same as Cannon." And so he dissolved my wrath.

I have always maintained that it is grossly unfair of owners to treat their jockeys more liberally than they do their trainers. For months before a big race the trainer is in a perpetual state of anxiety, and if he is able to present the horse at the post thoroughly fit the credit for the success which follows belongs mainly to him. The jockey can, and often does, undo in a minute the work of many weeks. I have nothing to say against the jockey being suitably rewarded, but the presents given are often beyond all reason, and cause a lot of mischief. It would, in my opinion, be far better for everybody concerned if there were a recognised and rigid scale of rewards both for jockeys and trainers. Some owners, I believe, make a practice of giving the trainer 10 per cent of the winnings. That is a liberal allowance. I think that if both the trainer and jockey received 5 per cent of the stakes won they would be fairly rewarded, and no present beyond that would be necessary. I can only say I wish I had been working under this arrangement during the time I was training. The value of the stakes won by horses I trained exceeded £70,000 (£56,000,000), and 5 per cent of that sum would have provided me with a comfortable fortune.

If I had been dependent, after my retirement, on the money I made by training horses I should have found myself a comparatively poor man. When he distributes largesse, an owner's first thought should be for his trainer, whereas it is almost invariably for the jockey. Hundreds of times an owner has come to me after we have won a race and asked, "What ought I to give the jockey?" It would rejoice me to know that I have been able to influence owners to think first of the claim of their trainers to suitable recognition.

113

Though the ground at Manchester was as hard as iron, Isonomy was none the worse for his effort there, and was "as fit as a fiddle" when he essayed the task of winning the Ascot Cup a second time. His opponents were Chippendale and Zut. The latter represented Count de Lagrange instead of Rayon d'Or, the winner of the St. Leger the previous year. The hopelessness of opposing Isonomy was evidently realised by Tom Jennings, who trained for the Count, and so Rayon d'Or was reserved for the Rous Memorial, decided an hour later, a race he duly won. In the contest for the Cup, Chippendale was allowed to make the running until inside the distance, but when given his head, Isonomy, on whom odds of 9 to 4 were laid, went to the front to win very comfortably.

The following year, 1881, Isonomy began his stud career at the Bonehill Paddocks, Tamworth, a fee of 50 guineas being charged for his services. A horse of his class begins nowadays at 300 guineas. He had won ten of his fourteen races, and been placed second twice and third once. The stakes he won amounted to £10,382 (£1,246,000). There were seven living foals resulting from his first season. It so happened that none of them won as a two-year-old in 1884 though Isobar scored pretty well afterwards. Not until 1887 did the son of Sterling establish his fame as a sire. That was the year Gallinule ran as a two-year-old. The following season came Satiety and Seabreeze; then, in succession, Riviera, Janissary, Common, Le Var, Prisoner, and finally Ravensbury and Isinglass.

Isonomy's offspring were racing during fourteen seasons, and in that period they won 254 races worth £205,032.

Isonomy had only been two years at the stud when Mr. Fred Gretton died. Sent by the executors to Tattersall's to be sold on New Year's Day, 1883 he was bought by Mr. Stirling Crawfurd (the husband of the Duchess of Montrose) for 9000 guineas, and was then transferred to the Bedford Lodge Stud at Newmarket, his fee being raised to 70 guineas. Presently he was moved to the Sefton Stud Farm, also at Newmarket. In 1889 his fee had gone up to £200, and he was advertised full for two years ahead. Sometime in 1884 the Duchess of Montrose asked the late Mr. Edmund Tattersall if he could find a buyer for Isonomy, as she was tired of the horse. Mr. Tattersall strongly advised her not to be in a hurry to part with him, and the wisdom of this counsel was proved within the next twelve months. Isonomy died of heart disease in 1891, the year after Isinglass and Ravensbury were born.

Isonomy was one of the foals got by Sterling in his first season, and the only one of that sire's stock to win as a two-year-old in 1877 though there were fifteen others. As a matter of fact, only three of the sixteen ever won—Isonomy, Lighthouse, and Sterlingworth. Isonomy's achievements sent Sterling's fee up from 100 to 150 guineas. It is, perhaps, worth noting that Isola Bella, the dam of Isonomy and Fernandez, was absolutely worthless as a racer. She was bred at Hooton by Mr. R. C. Naylor, whose colours she carried five times without once getting placed. In many works of reference Isola Bella is described as a bay; in reality she was a chestnut. Four of her seven foals were chestnuts, but Isonomy and Fernandez, the only two of any account, were both bays. Here is a summary of Isonomy's record as a sire of winners:

	Races Won.	Value		Races Won.	Value
1884			1892	21	£11,330
1885	11	£3,103	1893	23	26,410
1886	16	4,638	1894	25	42,056
1887	39	17,886	1895	27	20,342
1888	28	26,837	1896	5	2,458
1889	30	20,841	1897	2	283
1890	11	9,636			
1891	16	19,212	Totals	254	£205,032

In due course some of Isonomy's offspring came to Kingsclere to be trained, and most of them were endowed with pluck and determination, qualities which were so conspicuous in their sire. He was unquestionably one of the best horses I have ever known. I thought the world of him, and his achievements as a sire strengthened my regard and admiration.

In 1878 Fernandez, a brother to Isonomy, was one of the Yardley yearlings, and Mr. Fred Gretton bought him. He was a bay, but not a whole bay like Isonomy. Built on bigger lines than the latter, he was another "good one." A grand type of horse in every way, he was particularly powerful across the loins. He came slowly to hand and was unplaced in both the races he ran as a two-year-old. The following spring he won, to the surprise of most people, the Craven Stakes at Newmarket. Paddock critics declared him too "big," and odds of 15 to 1 were laid against him. He was however in much better condition than his appearance showed, and beat the favourite, Lord Falmouth's Merry-go-Round, a length and a half. A fortnight later we started both Fernandez and Mariner (another son of Sterling) for the Two Thousand Guineas. Mr. Gretton "declared" in favour of Mariner, but both ran unplaced. Fernandez's next outing was in the St. James's Palace Stakes at Ascot. I had no idea Mr. Gretton intended to run his horse that week, and he was not in racing trim. However, despite my expostulations, Mr. Gretton insisted that Fernandez should take his chance, and I was astounded when I saw him run the Derby winner, Bend Or, to a head at level weights. Those who had laid odds of 100 to 30 on Bend Or got a rare fright.

Fernandez was then put by for the Cambridgeshire. For that race he was handicapped at 8 st. 1 lb.; nevertheless, he started favourite at 9 to 2. Fordham rode him.

This autumn (writes Sir John Astley) I went for a big Stake on the Cambridgeshire, having got it into my head Fernandez was real good goods. . . . I never shall forget Gretton taking me into Fernandez's box the evening before the race. He had done himself a little extra well (as was not his unfrequent habit); and when I said I had never seen a horse look better, and that I considered the race as good as over, he replied, "Yes, that's all very well, but he has got at least ten pounds more on him than he would have had if Tom Cannon had not gone and run Bend Or to a head at Ascot. Whatever did he want to beat the Derby winner for ? I told him the horse wasn't fit, and that I wanted to win the Cambridgeshire with him." . . . And when I left him he (Gretton) was still bemoaning his jockey's uprightness over a glass of Scotch.

Fernandez was beaten half a length in the Cambridgeshire by Prince Soltykoff's Lucetta, a four-year-old to whom he was giving a stone. He had practically won the race when Lucetta swerved across the course on to him, and, to avoid knocking the mare over, Fordham had to check his horse. Immediately on returning to the Weighing-Room Fordham lodged an objection to Lucetta. Everybody assumed the Stewards would disqualify the winner; odds of 2 and 3 to 1 were laid on Fernandez getting the race. The inquiry into the affair was a most protracted one, and it was late in the evening before a decision was given. I was called as a witness, and ventured to express the opinion that whether Fernandez got the race or not he most certainly ought to. I was politely informed that that "was not evidence." While the inquiry was in progress I overheard a remark which forced me to believe the verdict would be against Fernandez. I reported this to Mr. Gretton and advised him to hedge his bets. He, however, refused to do so. The case against Lucetta was, he said, so strong that she must be disqualified. The Stewards, however, finally overruled the objection. The only explanation ever given for this unlooked-for, and, I venture to say, unjust, decision, is to be found in the *Reminiscences* of Sir George Chetwynd, who was one of the officiating Stewards. "Although," he writes, "she (Lucetta) had undoubtedly crossed Fernandez, it was a long way from home, and we thought Fordham had rather anticipated the swerving across him, and checked his horse so soon that there was plenty of time for him to have won his race afterwards if the horse had been good enough." It seems to me Sir George would have done well to act in accordance with the maxim that cautions a judge never to give a reason for his verdict. A more inconsequential argument than that he advances it would be difficult to conceive. Mr. Gretton naturally entertained a grievance against the Stewards, and few blamed him for so doing.

Mr. Gretton, however, seemed fated to be in " hot water." Before we had time to get over the annoyance caused by the result of the Cambridgeshire inquiry a more serious unpleasantness occurred in connection with the Liverpool Autumn Cup. Mr. Gretton had two horses in that event—Fernandez and Prestonpans.

The latter was a bay colt, three years old in 1880, by that remarkable horse Prince Charlie. The previous season, when the property of Lord Anglesey, Prestonpans showed some very useful form; so useful, indeed, that in the Royal Hunt Cup—his first race as a three-year-old, and the first in which he carried Mr. Gretton's colours—he was weighted 7 st. 10 lb. He ran "unplaced." His next race was the Liverpool Cup. Until almost the last moment I did not know whether I was to saddle Prestonpans or Fernandez. Nor did Mr. Gretton. At that time his betting interests were managed by Mr. Fred Swindell—"Lord Freddy" as his intimates generally called him—and when I went to

Liverpool he had not heard which of the two horses was carrying his money. The public assumed we should rely on Fernandez. They were wrong; Swindell backed Prestonpans, and Fernandez did not run. This policy infuriated the general body of backers, and after Prestonpans, ridden by Fordham, had won by half a length from Lord Drogheda's Philammon, with the Duke of Beaufort's Petronel third, a neck away, the crowd hooted and hissed viciously. There was a further hostile demonstration in the paddock while the horse passed through the throng on his way to the unsaddling enclosure.

This was a new and altogether disagreeable experience for me, and I need hardly say I left very much upset. I at once decided it was time Mr. Frederick Gretton and I parted company, and I asked him to be good enough to remove his horses from Kingsclere. Shortly afterwards I saw a string of the best-looking horses I had ever had in my stable march out of my yard. They went to old Alec Taylor. The yearlings which thus left me proved to be not so good as they looked, for I believe only one or two of them won races. It grieved me to have to lose the patronage of Mr. Gretton in this unceremonious fashion, but I could not afford to risk a repetition of that affair at Liverpool. I must add that I did not believe Mr. Gretton was, except indirectly, responsible for the manoeuvring that so incensed the public. He was a victim of the people who were pulling strings mainly to serve their own ends.

Fernandez remained in training two more seasons. As a four-year-old he started favourite for the Manchester Cup, but was unplaced, and then finished a poor third for the Goodwood Cup. At Goodwood he was quartered in the Duke of Richmond's stables. The Princess of Wales (Queen Alexandra) went round the stables one evening and expressed a desire to be shown "the fat horse." Everybody that week had been speaking of Fernandez as "the fattest horse they had ever seen." Rightly or wrongly, the idea prevailed that he was being reserved for the Cambridgeshire. If that actually was the plan it was abandoned, because no more was seen of Fernandez that season. The following year his only effort, and it was unsuccessful, was in the Royal Hunt Cup at Ascot. He was sold for 800 guineas on New Year's Day, 1883, when his brother Isonomy fetched 9000 guineas. There was, of course, no comparison between the two horses, and yet Fernandez was " good."

*　　*　　*

Conclusion by R.O.: Isonomy would almost certainly have won the Derby of 1878, had his participation been in accordance with the plans of his wildly volatile owner. In his absence, success went to William Stirling-Crawfurd's Sefton, one of the most moderate winners in the history of the race. After failing to win from four appearances as a two-year-old, he was beaten into second place in the Craven Stakes on reappearing at Newmarket the following spring, and did not strike winning form until he carried 5 st. 8 lbs. to scrape home by a head from Advance, who was giving him 34 lbs., in the City and Suburban Handicap at the Epsom April meeting. Sefton subsequently improved, but there is no case to be made out for his being a good horse, and he was a complete failure at stud, before being put down in 1891.

John Porter lived to see Isonomy become one of the most successful stallions in the country, as sire of the Triple Crown winners Common and Isinglass. One of the greatest horses of the century, Isinglass would never have been beaten but for temperament. Although as brave as all his breed, Isinglass thought of nothing but eating and sleeping, and never did a tap more than he had to on the course or on the gallops. After winning the St. Leger of 1893, Isinglass reverted to a mile and a quarter in the Lancashire Plate at Manchester. None of the other four jockeys were going to make running for him, and in a desperate attempt to capitalise stamina, Tommy Loates sent Isinglass on. It was a disaster. Finding himself with nothing against which to race, Isinglasss almost broke into a trot, and the wily Jack Watts got up on Raeburn to win an absolutely farcical race by a length, with La Fleche, winner of the One Thousand Guineas, the Oaks and St. Leger in 1892, third.

Mated with La Fleche, Isinglass became the sire of John O'Gaunt, who only won one race, the Hurstbourne Stakes worth £585 at the Bibury Club meeting at Salisbury, but ridden by amateur George Thursby was runner-up in the Two Thousand Guineas and Derby in 1904, and still more importantly maintained the great male dynasty of Isonomy.

In 1906 the sixteenth Earl of Derby sent his Oaks winner Canterbury Pilgrim to John O'Gaunt, and as a staunch Lancastrian, Lord Derby called the brown colt produced by that mating, Swynford after Catherine Swynford, mistress and third wife of John O'Gaunt, Duke of Lancaster, and ancestress of the Tudor kings. John Porter was 72 when

119

the boy jockey Frank Wootton rode the mighty Swynford to win the St. Leger of 1910 for the seventeenth Earl of Derby, but Porter was not to live to see the enormous influence which that great-grandson of Isonomy was to exert at stud. As well as the 1924 Derby winner, Sansovino, whom Tommy Weston rated the best horse he ever rode, Swynford got Blandford, who sired the Derby winners Trigo, Blenheim, Windsor Lad and Bahram.

Before being packed off to the United States by the late Aga Khan, Blenheim sired the high class Italian horse Donatello II. In 1936 Mr. Edward Esmond brought Donatello II to England, and in due course Donatello II sired the 1957 Derby winner Crepello and that splendid stayer Alycidon. Crepello became the sire of Busted, winner of the King George VI and Queen Elizabeth Stakes in 1967, and sire of Lady Beaverbrook's 1974 St. Leger winner Bustino. Bustino stands at the Royal Stud at Sandringham, and maintains the male line of Isonomy, whom the brewer saved for that gamble in the Cambridgeshire of 1878, rather than go for the jackpot in the Derby.

*   *   *

John Porter was born at Rugeley, Staffordshire, in 1838, when there were more racecourses in Staffordshire than in Yorkshire, and Hednesford, a few miles from Rugeley, was a thriving training centre. After being apprenticed to John Barham Day, in the Michel Grove stable near Findon in Sussex, and having only some twenty mounts in public, he became private trainer to to the Kentish baronet Sir Joseph Hawley in the Cannons Heath Stable in Hampshire at the age of only 25 in 1863. At the end of 1867 Porter moved into the Kingsclere Stable, which had been built by Sir Joseph, and the following year won the Derby for his patron with Blue Gown.

On the death of Sir Joseph Hawley in 1875, Porter exercised his option to buy Kingsclere for £4,000. One of the greatest trainers of the 19th century, though totally bereft of a sense of humour, Porter had the distinction of turning out three winners of the Triple Crown in Ormonde (1886) and Flying Fox (1899), both owned by the first Duke of Westminster, as well as with Common, owned in partnership by Lord Alington and Sir Frederick Johnstone, in 1891. In all John Porter saddled seven Derby winners at Epsom, a record for the race that still stands, as he was also responsible for the successes of the Duke of Westminster's Shotover in 1882, Sir Frederick Johnstone's St. Blaise in 1883 and Sir John Miller's Sainfoin in 1890.

John Porter retired at the end of 1905, and went to live in Ormonde House, now a College of Further Education, at Newbury. During 43 seasons he had won 1,063 races worth £720,021.

In retirement, John Porter founded and managed Newbury racecourse. When leaving Newbury on railway journeys to London, he had frequently looked at a level stretch of farmland to the east of the town, and reflected it would be an ideal site for a racecourse. On ascertaining that the owner Lloyd H. Baxendale of Greenham, was willing to sell, Porter drew up plans for a course, and submitted them to the Stewards of the Jockey Club, who dismissed them out of hand on the grounds that there were already sufficient courses.

As he left the Jockey Club Rooms, Porter met King Edward VII, who asked him what he had been doing. On Porter explaining how he had been badly disappointed by the Stewards, the King asked to see the plans, and being impressed by the scheme, undertook to raise the matter with the Jockey Club. On a second, and very much more cordial, meeting with the Stewards of the Jockey Club, John Porter received an immediate promise of a licence for a new racecourse at Newbury.

The inaugural meeting at Newbury was held on 26th and 27th September 1905. Three of the races were won by the local owner Lord Carnarvon, of Highclere Castle, whose grandson, the present Earl, is chairman of Newbury Racecourse Company as well as the Queen's Racing Manager.

John Porter, who should have won an eighth Derby with Isonomy, died in 1922.

A RINGER AT CHELTENHAM'S 1919 NEW YEAR MEETING

(Peter Christian Barrie, King of the Ringers)

Introduction by R.O.: As racing got back into full swing after the end of the First World War, thousands of servicemen flocked to the racecourses, determined to enjoy themselves at last, after the misery and mud of the trenches. With their gratuities to finance them they enjoyed the exhilaration of attacking the bookmakers, instead of the Boche. After early reverses the ANZAC member of the Australia and New Zealand Army Corps, Peter Barrie took elaborate measures to protect his investments. Unfortunately, what might have passed muster in the Bush, did not commend itself to the Courts of Law or the Jockey Club.

*   *   *

John Welcome, the acknowledged expert on legal proceedings arising from malpractice on the racecourse, gives a detailed account of the nefarious operations of the notorious 'Ringer' Barrie.

*   *   *

Peter Christian Barrie was one of the most audacious, convincing and, for a time, successful of all the many crooks and swindlers who have trod the English Turf. Barrie was born in the Australian outback of English parents and, like many of his countrymen who hailed from those wide open spaces, was an accomplished horseman and horsemaster with an eye for a horse and, in addition, an instinctive ability to sense where one could be successfully substituted for another. It was this latter which earned for him before the law caught up with him, the title 'King of the Ringers,' and he was forever known, after he had done his term in prison and returned to the Turf, as 'Ringer Barrie.'

123

him, the title 'King of the Ringers,' and he was forever known, after he had done his term in prison and returned to the Turf, as 'Ringer Barrie.'

Barrie had served with the Australian Light Horse in Gallipoli during the First World War, had been wounded and returned to England, and passed as unfit for further service. There he immediately plunged into various activities on the Turf. By 1919, like all the best confidence tricksters, the appearance he presented to the world was one of prosperity. His suits came from Savile Row, his shirts from Jermyn Street, he had a suite at the Queen's Hotel in Leicester Square, and eight horses in training, some of which he rode himself not without success. But it was all a sham. By the autumn of 1919 his credit had run out and he was broke.

Barrie was a man of considerable charm by which he could persuade others to his will, he had an ingenious turn of mind, was completely without scruple and possessed of an effrontery of such magnitude that it enabled him to take risks reckless in the extreme and get away with them - for a time. He had already experimented successfully with dope or 'hurry-up powders' as he dubbed them, but in October 1919 with creditors pressing on every side, he decided to go for bigger things, run a ringer at Stockton and bring off a really telling coup. In his string was a two-year-old called Coat of Mail which had proved so useless that even those 'hurry-up' powders had failed to bring him home. However Barrie now determined to turn his lack of form to good account by substituting a good three-year-old for him in a juvenile race at Stockton. Looking about for a likely candidate for such a substitution he found one in Jazz, a colt then owned by Sir Hedworth Meux and trained by Atty Persse which he knew was for sale. He arranged for Hopkins, an associate of his, to buy Jazz and the deal was concluded at Newbury races on October 22nd. The price was £800 with a stipulation that the horse was not to run again in England which made him exactly suited to Barrie's plan. He promptly entered Coat of Mail for the Faceby Plate at Stockton using the assumed name of 'A.Pearson' and the entry was accepted.

Jazz was duly handed over in London and Barrie travelled with him in the railway horse box to Stockton. There, being well aware of the real Coat of Mail's contours, colour and appearance, he carried out an art he was later to perfect - that of making one horse resemble another by use of paint and dye. Because of Coat of Mail's total lack of form he expected a long price and he got it. Coat of Mail opened at 20-1 but such was the weight of money poured on him by Barrie and Hopkins, who was in on the secret, that he rapidly shortened to favourite at 9-2 in a field of eight. No jockey had been engaged by Barrie before the race since he feared that if it became known that a prominent jockey had been engaged the price might shorten but, once on the course finding that Billy Griggs, a prominent rider of the time, was without a ride in the race, he approached him. Reluctant at first when he saw that the price was tumbling down Griggs agreed to take the mount. So sure of the outcome was Barrie that he did not bother to administer any of his 'hurry-up' powders. "Never dope a horse that can do it without," was, he averred, one of his maxims. The deception, too, was assisted by the fact that flurries of snow were driving across the course and enclosures during the afternoon which deterred anyone from taking a closer look at Coat of Mail which was in any event rugged up until the last minute.

When Griggs asked for instructions Barrie, not wishing to publicise his win, told him to lie handy and come away to win by one or two lengths, but in fact Griggs jumped him out of the gate, was never headed and won as he liked, thus attracting all the attention Barrie did not want. "That's not a horse, it's an aeroplane," someone in the crowd shouted as he passed the post. "That's the best two-year-old I've ever ridden," Griggs told him. "What's he worth?"

"Thousands", answered Barrie happily, and indeed he was to him - then. Just how much he took out of the ring has never been accurately disclosed but it is thought to have been in the region of £10,000, approximately £450,000 in today's money. But certain of the more acute of the racing press were curious.

One of their more telling comments was: "Coat of Mail's connections were not entertaining an angel unawares." And Barrie, reckless as ever, over-played his hand. He pocketed the takings and refused to give Hopkins and the shipper who had been engaged as an extra bluff to transport the horse to India and who had rashly been let into the secret, their agreed shares of the loot. They protested but to no avail and then they talked. Soon it was all around racing circles that Barrie had brought off a great coup with a ringer at Stockton. Meeting an acquaintance in London a little later he tapped Barrie on the waistcoat saying, "That's a nice coat of mail you have on. Have you had it dyed?"

Due to the attention drawn to the affair by the talk and press comment, Weatherby's wrote to 'A.Pearson' asking for an explanation. In reply they received a letter from Barrie signed 'A.Pearson' cleverly constructed to erect a smokescreen over the matter and giving them no real information at all. Apparently satisfied with this Weatherby's paid out the stake money. This convinced Barrie he had got clean away with it but he was wrong. After sitting on the matter for some time Weatherby's, under pressure from more and wilder rumours and press comment, called in Scotland Yard.

Unaware of this and even if he had been, unlikely to have paid any attention to it, Barrie was planning an even more audacious coup. He had in his wife's name a mare called Shining More which he had purchased in September when he was temporarily in funds for eight hundred guineas with a view to exploiting her. Delighted with the success of the Coat of Mail affair, his fertile mind devised a way of doing this and, he hoped, keeping his name out of the plot. Her next race, he decided, would be in the Malvern Selling Hurdle at Cheltenham on December 29th but she would not run as Shining More nor in his name.

A man called Cyril Lawley who ran the Silver Badge Motor Works at Hampstead was a friend of Barrie's and the two of them agreed to enter her as Silver Badge, claiming her to have been bought cheaply at a sale of army remounts. The letter entering her and explaining this, composed in Barrie's best style appeared to Weatherby's to be 'quite straightforward and innocent', and was swallowed whole by them, perhaps assisted by the fact that it was signed *C.Lawley. Lieut* R.E. It should perhaps be stated here that Lawley, somewhat improbably, protested throughout the later proceedings that he had been completely taken in by Barrie and acted only as a naive dupe.

Barrie was now confronted by the fact that the description given to Weatherby's in the letter entering her in no way corresponded with the real Shining More. They had described her as a brown mare, pedigree unknown, no markings, whilst Shining More was a striking bay mare with a white blaze and a white hind fetlock and, moreover, was well scrutinising the runners. None of this interrupted Barrie's plans or shook his nerve. After comparing the two horses carefully he set to work. Having obtained a new and stronger dye he painted Shining More all over until she became brown taking care to heavily cover the blaze and fetlock. He also pulled and trimmed her tail and to add further verisimilitude to the story of her coming from a remount sale he singed the army brand on her quarters and 'lightly burned' army numbers and a broad arrow on her hoofs. Further to assist and complicate the plot he entered the real Shining More in the next race under her own name. It was not, of course, intended that she would run. It is a tribute to Barrie's skill that Gwilt, when this 'army cast-off' was brought into the ring, strode over to have a good look at her and totally failed to recognise his former charge.

To ride the well publicised 'army remount' Barrie engaged Tom Hulme, a leading hurdle jockey, who, when he saw her markings expressed in no uncertain terms his disgust at being put on such a hair-trunk. He laughed at Barrie when Barrie told him she would win but his scorn turned to wonder when she came home cantering at 10-1, Barrie and his accomplices having backed her down from 20-1 and netted the nice sum of £7,000 (£224,000).

This time the coup appeared complete. Even *The Sporting Life* accepted the 'remount' story saying she, 'was at the Shirehampton Remount Depot before Mr. C.S. Lawley purchased her at the army sale in Bristol on March 18th for, it is said, only 19 gns...' Barrie therefore could compliment himself on having cleverly covered his tracks and those of his associates. But behind the scenes the C.I.D were at work and their enquiries amongst the rougher fringe of racing regulars led them inexorably towards Barrie who, alerted now, began to scent danger. Immediately he set to work to get rid of the two fictitious horses, Coat of Mail and Silver Badge.

The first difficulty which confronted him was the cleansing of the dye which he described as 'a new American mouth wash' from Shining More. He had done his work almost too well. It took him two days, much peroxide and all his ingenuity in fending off enquiries from those anxious to learn more and inspect this extraordinary army reject which had turned into a flying machine. Eventually the net closed and he and his accomplices were arrested. The trial took nineteen days. Hopkins, his accomplices were arrested. The trial took nineteen days. Hopkins, whom the judge described as having no proper sense of right or wrong when dealing with horses, was given fifteen months imprisonment without hard labour. Lawley was lucky to have his plea in mitigation that he was an innocent dupe largely accepted and was only fined £100. Barrie, the brains and the instigator, went down for three years with hard labour. He has been described as 'a thumping crook' which he was, but he deserves some sort of Turf immortality for the answer he gave the examining magistrate when asked what he considered a good thing in racing. His effrontery and cheek never deserted him even when in the dock. "A useful three-year-old in a moderate two-year-old, your honour," was his reply.

*   *   *

Conclusion by R.O.: There can be no gain in saying that the enlightenment that 'Ringer' Barrie offered the bench, when he declared that a useful three-year-old in a moderate two-year-old race was a good bet. Had Jazz been qualified for that race at Stockton, and been allowed to appear in his own identity, he would have had to give the other runners 20 lbs. according to the official weight-for-age scales. As 3 lbs. is reckoned to be the equivalent of a length, that means he enjoyed the equivalent of almost seven lengths start, when he landed that coup for Barrie. No wonder Billy Griggs said that he was the best two-year-old he had ever ridden!

Jazz was still a maiden when he ran at Stockton as Coat of Mail, but was palpably useful. On 21st August he had run Woorali to three parts of a length over five furlongs at Stockton, and eight days later he was only beaten a short head by Little Cell at the end of six furlongs at Gatwick. Sir Headworth Meux, from whom he was obtained, was a brother of the Hon. George Lambton. He changed his name on inheriting the fortune of Lady Meux, the widow of a brewer of Friary Meux fame, with a penchant for handsome young men. Like all of his family, Hedworth Lambton fitted that particular bill to perfection. Fortunately for him, the fickle Lady Meux died before she met another Adonis, and changed not only her mind but her will as well.

128

Soon after completing his sentence, 'Ringer' Barrie disappeared from the Turf with the same suddenness as he had arrived. Rogue though he may have been, he was a bold and amusing one.

Billy Griggs was thirty six years old when he rode the spurious Coat of Mail to win at Stockton. Born at New Brompton on 11th May 1883, he was apprenticed to Bob Sherwood the younger in the St. Gatien stable, now occupied by Robert Armstrong, at Newmarket. In 1904 he won both the Chester Cup on Sandboy and the Stewards Cup on Melayr, then the following year the Lincolnshire on Sansovino, obtaining his only Classic success on Cinna in the One Thousand Guineas in 1920. On retiring from the saddle, he began training in 1923, and returned to Stockton to saddle his first winner, Soulector.

Every winter, Billy Griggs used to go to Switzerland, where he died during a game of curling at the age of eighty eight in 1972.

*   *   *

John Welcome is the doyen of racing historians. Among his most important books are *Fred Archer* (Faber & Faber, 1967), an outstanding biography of the greatest of the Victorian jockeys, and *Neck or Nothing,* an account of the extraordinary life of the professional gambler Bob Sievier, who owned and trained the great mare Sceptre, winner of the One Thousand Guineas, Two Thousand Guineas, Oaks and St. Leger in 1902. The Archer biography was published in a revised edition, with a foreword by Lester Piggott, as *Fred Archer, A Complete Study,* by Lambourn Press in 1990.

The first contribution to the literature of the Turf that John made was *The Cheltenham Gold Cup* (Constable, 1957), the story of the great steeplechase, which went into a second edition, when brought up to date. He is also the author of *Grand National,* a best selling novel published by Hamish Hamilton in 1976, and as a paperback by Sphere Books in 1977. In collaboration with Rupert Collens he has written three brilliant books on *Snaffles,* the equine artist, Charlie Johnson Payne (1884-1967).

In addition to his books on racing, John Welcome has written several of general and legal interest, besides editing a number of anthologies.

A former Chairman and Steward of the Irish National Hunt Committee, he has been fascinated by racing and hunting for more than sixty years. He lives in Co. Wexford.

130

JOHN HISLOP LANDS A LAMBTON GAMBLE - JUST!

(How Big Ben Beat Prominent Lad
At Newbury In 1939)

Introduction by R.O.: The Hon. George Lambton was born in 1860, the fifth son of the second Earl of Durham. He was never a rich man, and frequently a poor one. Dapper and always immaculately dressed, he was of distinctly handsome appearance with large brown eyes and neat, regular features, beneath crisp brown hair.

In his younger days he was a brilliant amateur rider, both on the flat and over fences, relying then, as he would do for the rest of his life, on successful punting to keep body and soul together. Despite his having some of the best horses of the century through his hands he always lived a long way above his income. In 1888 he won the Grand Steeplechase de Paris on Parasang, but his career in the saddle was brought to an end by the heavy fall he took on Hollington at Sandown Park in February, 1892.

For several years George Lambton was virtually a cripple. All the same he began training with a small string at Newmarket, thereby starting a minor social revolution, as hitherto the running of a racing stable had been regarded as an unsuitable occupation for members of the aristocracy or gentry. The opening of a stable by George Lambton can be said to have been the first step towards training becoming a profession, rather than a trade.

In 1893 George Lambton accepted the offer to become private trainer to the sixteenth Earl of Derby who was reviving the family's racing interests and building the beautiful Stanley House stable at Newmarket. Lord Derby died in 1908 and was succeeded by his eldest son, for whom Lambton won the Derby with Sansovino in 1924 and Hyperion in 1933. At the end of 1933, however, the seventeenth Earl of Derby, grandfather of the present peer, caused a sensation by announcing that the forty years of association between his family and George Lambton had come to an end. In the opinion of Lord Derby, Lambton, at the age of seventy three, was too old to carry the responsibilities of running a large stable. Lambton was furious.

With bitter reproach he wrote to Lord Derby, pointing out that he was being given just six weeks notice, sarcastically enquiring whether it was a record. He went on to point out that throughout the autumn they had been discussing the new intake of yearlings, and the entries that would have to be made for them, yet in his heart Lord Derby knew that he was going to have nothing at all to do with them. While deeply hurt, George Lambton assured the man that he had served faithfully for four decades that he had no intention of retiring.

As good as his word George Lambton moved out of Stanley House, into Kremlin House, now the quarters of Michael Jarvis. By 1935 he had forty five horses in the yard, a huge string by the standards of those days; the owners including his brother Brigadier Charles Lambton and his nephew the fifth Earl of Durham, together with Major Dermot McCalmont, Lord Hamilton of Dalzell and Lord Queenborough. As well as the Chester Cup with Damascus, George Lambton won the Victoria Cup with Precious Pearl and the Queen's Prize with Apple Peel that season. Apple Peel was ridden by his apprentice Bill Rickaby, whose father and paternal grandfather had both been stable jockey to Lambton at Stanley House.

Having taken out a licence to train jumpers to oblige George Lambton and his family, as related by John Hislop below, Tom Masson very soon built up a useful stable and had a string of eighteen horses in 1939. As well as with Damascus, whom John Hislop rode to success in the Coventry Novices Chase at Cheltenham, he won with a number of other horses during that last pre-war jumping season of 1938/9. Sad Jester won two races over fences at Lingfield and another at Newbury, Kiddie Sister and Cuban Cabby both won over hurdles at Wye, Berks and Bucks and John Peel scored over hurdles at Fontwell and Gatwick respectively, while Scotch Woodcock, with John Hislop up, was successful over hurdles at Birmingham. Stethoscope, also ridden by John Hislop, won a hurdle at Lingfield.

A cheerful well-built man with bushy grey eyebrows, Tom Masson was born in 1898 the son of a Scottish farmer. Having a natural affinity with animals originating from his upbringing amongst livestock, he was already an accomplished horseman in boyhood. During the early part of his life he enjoyed widespread recognition for the schooling of showjumpers who achieved success in the highest class, while his equine experience also included an important spell of close involvement with the horses in Bertram Mills circus before John Hislop persuaded him to turn his talents to the training of racehorses.

*   *   *

John Hislop belongs to that very select group of men who have ever been able to give an absolutely first hand account of a race, by reason of his having the talent to write as well as he used to ride on the flat and under National Hunt Rules. As well as being a writer and rider, he is conversant with all other aspects of racing, from designing the matings of high class stock, to the plotting of a horse's long term programme, adjudication in the Stewards' Room - and bringing off a betting coup. Here, he tells how he masterminded a gamble that produced a gratefully received windfall for George Lambton and family.

*   *   *

One day in 1938, George Lambton asked me if I knew anyone good at schooling horses, as he had two geldings which he thought would benefit from being taught to jump.

One was a horse called Damascus, a useful handicapper and a winner of the Chester Cup, who had become so nappy that he would not go on to Newmarket Heath; the other, Big Ben, had been bought for George's second son, Teddy, to hunt and ride in point-to-points, but had proved an erratic and sketchy jumper.

At that time I was a pupil with the trainer, Victor Gilpin, at the Clarehaven Stable in Newmarket and he had introduced me to a man called Tom Masson, a fine horseman from whom Victor had bought several first-class hunters. I became a close friend of Tom Masson, who was particularly adept at teaching horses to jump and straightening out difficult or intractable individuals. Tom was then farming in Hertfordshire, near Welwyn Garden City, and I often went over to school horses under his direction and learn all I could from him about practical horsemanship.

When George Lambton approached me about someone who could deal with Damascus and Big Ben, Tom Masson immediately came to mind. I recommended Tom to Mr. Lambton and the two horses were sent to him immediately.

Soon both horses were going and jumping so well that Tom remarked to me that he thought each could win under National Hunt Rules. I reported this to the Lambtons who went over to Tom's farm to see how the horses performed. They were so pleased with what they saw that George Lambton arranged for Tom to take charge of Damascus and Big Ben. As a result, Tom gave up farming and moved to the Barn Stables at Lewes - long since demolished - across the road from Lewes Gaol, where he remained for the rest of his life until he died as the result of a car accident some years after the last war.

To my great joy, the Lambtons most kindly asked me to ride both horses in their races. This story only concerns Big Ben, an eight-year-old bred at the Swynford Paddocks Stud near Newmarket.

Big Ben was a tall, rangy, ugly horse, a dirty chestnut in colour. He had a big bold, plain head, a good eye, lean neck, fine shoulder, deep girth, though running up rather light behind the saddle, powerful quarters and strong limbs, but unattractive curly hocks. In addition he was a crib biter, wind-sucker and weaver.

Despite his flaws, Big Ben had a certain presence about him: a noble, courageous outlook and a kind, gentle nature. His pedigree was that of a flat racehorse, being by the Derby winner Papyrus out of Madame Sans Gene, by March Along out of Assurance, by Count Schomberg out of Be Sure, dam of Stedfast, a good racehorse who finished second to Sunstar in the Derby of 1911 and later became a successful sire.

Something must have gone awry in Big Ben's genetic make-up since he bore no resemblance to his sire, Papyrus, a neat horse of fine quality, nor to a flat racehorse in general. Due to his size, backwardness and lack of quality he was probably gelded at an early stage and put by as a store, because he never raced on the flat.

When Big Ben went into training to race under National Hunt Rules, he showed that his early schooling to jump had not been wasted. When faced with steeplechase fences at racing pace on the schooling ground, he dealt with them efficiently, boldly and accurately. His work on the flat showed him to be an impressive, resolute galloper, partial to soft ground and likely to stay well. It was decided to lay Big Ben out for a gamble in a Selling Handicap 'Chase

Since he was un-raced, Big Ben had to have three runs before he was eligible to be given anything less than top weight in a handicap. His first appearance was on December 8th, 1938 at Gatwick, now the site of the airport in a 3 mile selling Handicap 'Chase in which he automatically carried 12 st. 7 1bs.. There were seven runners, the favourite being a useful plater over fences, Diabutsu, who duly won by ten lengths. Big Ben, at 100 - 7 others, gave me a dreadful ride. He pulled like a train and hung so badly that he appeared to have only one side to his mouth, making him difficult to steer. Gatwick was a testing course - the fences were big and stiff and the going, being clay, got very holding after rain. However, Big Ben jumped magnificently and, allowing for the ground he gave away by hanging so badly, he ran a pretty good race. He raced in Teddy Lambton's name and carried the family colours of pale blue with a brown cap.

In an attempt to make Big Ben easier to ride, Tom Masson decided to see how he went in a chain-snaffle, the bit consisting of large chain links. This proved to be the key to his mouth; in it he neither pulled nor hung and seemed to find it to his liking.

Big Ben's next race was six days later in a similar event to the first, this time at Windsor, where the fences were considerably easier than at Gatwick. There were twelve runners and again Diabutsu was favourite, but he blundered his chance away and finished sixth, the winner being Grangefield, a firm second favourite.

Big Ben's third run was once more at Gatwick in a Selling Handicap 'Chase over three miles, in which he was still weighed at 12 st. 7 1bs.. Also at 12 st. 7 1bs. was Prominent Lad, who had previously run fourth in the Lingfield Open Handicap 'Chase over three miles and although receiving weight all round, he was in a lighter class in that race than he would have been in a Seller.

However, Prominent Lad failed to concede the 'professional plater' Diabutsu, 13 1bs. and was beaten five lengths by him. Of the other runners, two who were winners last time out fell and another was pulled up. This left Big Ben with only one opponent, apart from the leading pair, who was stone cold. As a result, Big Ben finished third, at which Tom Masson was far from pleased in view of Big Ben's future handicapping and as I came in he observed to me icily, "do you see where you are?". His irritation was understandable. In those days the rules governing race riding were more flexible than they are now, and if a jockey saw that he could not win, it was permissible for him to pull the horse out of the race. In fact a rider's orders often were: "Win if you can, but if you can't, try not to be in the first three!". Today this would entail an immediate summons before the Stewards.

As it was, I had little option but to be anywhere else. Big Ben, who started at 20 - 1, finishing two lengths behind Prominent Lad. The three races necessary to earning a handicap mark, other than top weight, having been completed, we waited anxiously to discover the handicapper's view of Big Ben.

He was entered in the Royston Selling Handicap 'Chase, two-and-a-half miles at Newbury, a galloping course with good big fences which we thought would suit him. The distance of two-and-a-half miles, as opposed to three miles, was chosen because while it was absolutely certain that Big Ben stayed the distance, his ability to see out a strongly run three miles to the bitter end had not yet been proven.

When the weights came out it was seen that Prominent Lad, with 12 st. was set to give Big Ben 5 lbs.. At 11 st. 9 lbs., it could not be said that Big Ben was thrown in, since he was giving weight to nearly all the entries, but these were no more than run out of the mill platers, while Big Ben had improved markedly with each race and could have finished closer to Prominent Lad at Gatwick. With the advantage of 5 lbs., we were sure that Big Ben would beat Prominent Lad and that the other entries were not good enough to trouble us.

Prominent Lad was trained by Jack Anthony, a great steeplechase rider in his day, but as a trainer not in the same class as his brother Ivor, who was outstanding. A strong, compact, well-balanced, medium sized chestnut gelding, Prominent Lad was consistent and a good jumper, but no more than a plater, if a useful one. He ran in blinkers which may have indicated idleness or cunning - or both - and was usually ridden by Jack Moloney, a superb rider and one of the best never to win a Grand National.

By this time Victor Gilpin had moved from Newmarket to Michel

Grove near Arundel. This enabled me to ride out regularly with Tom Masson at Lewes, all winter, getting to know Big Ben well.

Big Ben's race at Newbury was on January 20th, 1939 and we decided that this was to be 'D' Day. Always a cautious gambler, I arranged to have £100 (a quarter of my annual income) in the stable commission. The rest of the investment was far greater, so that Big Ben finally started favourite at 2 - 1 with Prominent Lad next at 6 - 1

Some thirty years ago, I wrote an account of the race in a book, *Far From a Gentleman* and can do no better than to return to it now:

"As I drove to Newbury on the day, I felt an unusual sense of excitement - the feeling which the approaching realisation of a carefully planned and prepared operation arouses in the individual responsible for its conception and undertaking, whether he is the commander of an armed force or a burglar. There are doubtless many who will consider the latter the more appropriate similie.

A thin, cold rain was falling - it always seemed to be raining on days of eventful races in my career - and in spite of my usual nervous irritability, I felt calm and confident. In some ways a good deal of responsibility lay upon me: recommending the Lambtons to send the horses to Tom, designing and carrying out the plan of campaign and, finally, being the one upon whom the entire outcome of the operation depended.

While my character, physique and riding ability left much to be desired, I was never overawed by the importance of the occasion: the more that depended upon me the less erratic my judgment; and the idea of riding a well-backed horse was strangely stimulating.

Though Big Ben was the last type of horse to appeal to me - I have always preferred medium-sized horses of quality to big, plain, coarse ones - I had grown fond of him. He had all the courage in the world, loved his job, which he knew inside out, and would never fail you. Small, easy fences he would treat like hurdles, but without giving his rider a qualm; big, stiff ones, as at Gatwick or Newbury, he regarded as a challenge to his power - when he saw one of these ahead he would take a fresh hold of his bit, prick his ears, lengthen his stride and bear down on it with a will. If he met a fence right he would stand back in the wings, reach for it and skim the top, landing with yards to spare. If he found himself out of his stride, was hampered or unsighted, he remained unperturbed, fitting his actions to the circumstances by putting in a short one, taking off blind or, if the worst came to the worst and he knew he was going to hit the obstacle, checking himself slightly so that, as a skilled boxer rides a punch, the impact did not impair his balance. However hard he was ridden into a fence he never lost his head, the perfection and reliability of his performance reflecting the thoroughness and skill with which Tom had schooled him. I greatly looked forward to the first real test of Big Ben's merit.

'You don't look too good mate', Frenchie Nicholson remarked to me as we hung about before the start, waiting to come under orders. As it was still raining, I had not been warmed up by a previous ride and the nervous tension of the occasion was becoming acute. I can well believe that there were grounds for his observations.

'Don't feel too good. We've got the lot on today and I can't wait to get it over.'

'I know the feeling. Anyway, it won't be long now.'

As this exchange of niceties ended we came under orders; and the starter, doubtless being as anxious to return to the warmth of the weighing room as we were to get on with the job, sent us off.

I settled Big Ben down in the middle of the field and went quietly round. A couple of horses fell at the water in front of the stands, but did not interfere with us. After half way I gradually improved our position and as we entered the straight we moved up to share the lead with Prominent Lad and Jack Moloney. The rest of the field had dropped back into oblivion in the mist and the rain.

Big Ben was going so well that I felt certain he would win, but all up the straight Prominent Lad stuck with him. Big Ben was jumping superbly, standing right back at each fence, so that I had hopes that, by luring Prominent Lad into trying to do the same, we might jump him down. Prominent Lad was too cunning to fall for this ruse, and though we gained at each jump, his blinkered head would draw level before we reached the next, his short, scuffling gait contrasting markedly with Big Ben's giant stride. Out of the corner of my eye I glimpsed Jack Moloney's immobile, yellowish, almost oriental features, stamped by the set of his eyebrows with a faint expression of permanent surprise.

As imperturbable as he was stylish and secure, Jack Moloney was a beautiful rider over fences, with so delicate a touch of hand that he could have ridden round Aintree with paper reins. It was impossible to tell from his face how he was going.

Coming into the last fence I felt confident that Big Ben had the race won, and when he landed half-a-length clear it seemed that the battle was virtually over. But suddenly he appeared to stick in the mud, as if he had run into a piece of false going, and to my horror and anguish, Prominent Lad shot by to gain a length lead.

In this brief fragment of time my elation plunged into despair. The outlook seemed utterly hopeless. I gave Big Ben a couple of strides to regain the rhythm of his gallop - a horse may make up lost ground if he is balanced for his finishing run; he will never do so if he is not - and Prominent Lad stole another half-length. Then Big Ben started in pursuit, fruitless though it looked.

There is this about horses of true courage and resolution: they will inspire a rider with a sense of hope when all hope has gone, and will demoralise an opponent by the relentless determination with which they refuse to accept defeat. And as Big Ben found the full momentum of his stride and set about renewing the battle, the outlook suddenly brightened. I felt a pang of shame that the very idea of defeat should have shadowed my thoughts. At Tattersalls he had drawn up to Prominent Lad's girths, at the Members he was only a neck behind. With twenty yards to go he still had a head to make up, but in those last few strides he stuck out his nose and put all his great heart into one final effort. This late and unexpected challenge was too much for Prominent Lad: instead of diving for the finishing line with the determination of a true battler, he surrendered.

It was too close a thing to be sure which had won, though a stride past the post Big Ben was a neck to the good. When we were pulling up, I strained my ears to try to catch the numbers as they were given out but the wind turned the loudspeaker into a meaningless distortion.

It was only as I rode back to the paddock and saw the number in the frame that the result showed our victory assured. And, as every jockey who has experienced those agonising moments of uncertainty will appreciate, all the cares of eternity seemed to have been lifted from my mind. My mount had won by a short head."

Big Ben was bought in for the reasonable sum of 210 guineas, and went on to win four of his remaining races, another seller at Gatwick and non-selling handicaps at Plumpton (twice) and Newton Abbot. His only defeat was by a useful horse called Straight Larch at Hawthorn Hill in an Open Handicap.

I never rode Big Ben again after that season, being in France with the Sussex Yeomanry, the war having started. He won one more race, a seller at Windsor, ridden by Don Butchers, was later retired and put down when National Hunt racing ceased for a time during the war.

Of all Big Ben's victories, the one which really mattered was the Royston Selling Handicap 'Chase at Newbury on the 20th of January, 1938.

*   *   *

Conclusion by R.O.: George Lambton, who had been responsible

139

for the purchase of Big Ben, obtained his final success with Golden Cloud, later a notable sire of sprinters, at Newmarket on 9th June 1945. Finally, after a career spanning fifty two years, he retired on 21st July 1945. Two days later he died.

George Lambton remained a bachelor until he was forty eight, then in 1908 he married Cicely Horner, the beautiful, statuesque daughter of Sir John Horner whose ancestral home was Mells Manor in Somerset. Cicely's sister Katherine was the wife of Raymond Asquith, son of the Prime Minister, Herbert Asquith. George Lambton's brother-in-law Raymond Asquith, was killed leading a charge of the Third Grenadier Guards on the Western front on 15th July, 1916.

The second son of George and Cicely Lambton was Edward George Lambton, who took over the Kremlin House stable, on demobilisation from the Royal Horse Guards in 1945. Handsome, urbane and elegant, Teddy Lambton had many things in common with his father, as he also had an uncanny understanding of the thoroughbred, and bet very heavily indeed, often being in extremely deep water financially.

At the outset of his training career, things went well for Teddy. He brought off the first major gamble of the post-war era when the stable backed Mr. Tom Best's Langton Abbot down to 7 - 1 clear favourite in a field of thirty seven for the Lincolnshire of 1946, and ridden by Tommy Weston, the four-year-old won by a very easy four lengths. A little over four months later they had another touch when Mr. H. E. 'Manna' Morris's filly Foxtrot readily justified favouritism for the Ebor Handicap. Over the next year or two, their luck changed. The bookmakers recovered their losses with compound interest, and in 1949, Teddy was obliged to give them a rest for the time being by handing in his licence.

By 1961, Teddy was able to resume training in a modest way, with ten horses, all belonging to his mother, in the Kremlin yard. None of the old Lambton touch had been lost. Compensation won the Imperial Stakes, at the time a race of some consequence and two other events, while Avec La Table, also a two-year-old, won a couple of times. The following season, Compensation was successful in the Cork and Orrery Stakes at Royal Ascot.

The Kremlin string had grown to forty by the outset of the 1964 season, Miss Monica Sheriffe, Mr. R. C. Boucher and other well known owners having joined the stable. That year Teddy was responsible for Mighty Gurkha winning the Lincolnshire, the last time it was run on its original site at Lincoln before being transferred to Doncaster, and in the autumn the Ayr Gold Cup was won by Compensation, whose paternal grandsire was Golden Cloud. Three years later, in 1967, Teddy performed a feat of typical Lambton brilliance by winning nine consecutive races with the two-year-old Kursaal. Owned and bred by his mother, Kursaal was a wonderfully well named chestnut, the daughter of Vienna and Avec la Table, who also had Golden Cloud for a maternal grandsire. There was nothing about the Golden Cloud clan that Teddy did not know or understand.

An insouciantly charming as ever, Teddy was now firmly re-established amongst leading trainers, and in 1968 he won the Wokingham Stakes with the late Phil Bull's Charicles at Royal Ascot, as well as more than twenty other races. All the same the clouds were gathering again, and difficulties accumulating. In 1969 Teddy called a Compensation filly, which he owed in partnership with his mother, Collateral, remarking to me that the only way he could obtain collateral as security for a loan, was by using it as a name for a horse. His luck was not going to change a second time though, and on 14th August 1969, Teddy again relinquished his licence to train, handing over the Kremlin yard to his stable jockey Peter Robinson, father of that fine rider of the present time, Peter Robinson.

Until the end of his life, Teddy Lambton was one of the most popular personalities at Newmarket. He was only sixty five when he died after a short illness in June 1983.

Cicely Lambton survived her husband by twenty seven years, being about ninety at the time of her death in December 1972. Throughout a close association with racing that began in the Edwardian era, she was a quite fearless punter. One of her most memorable touches was over Scotch Woodcock when he was ridden by John Hislop at Birmingham.

Having obtained his earliest training success with Big Ben, Scotch Woodcock and other jumpers owned by the Lambton family in 1939, Tom Masson received widespread recognition after the war. In 1960 the Queen sent him two horses, one of whom, Gallega, became the first Royal winner of the season. The same year he won both the Ascot Stakes and the Brown Jack Stakes with Shatter. Two years later he won the Lingfield Derby Trial Stakes with Mr. A. B. Askew's Pindaric, who was brought down in the Derby.

The death of Tom Masson occurred a matter of months after Teddy Lambton finally retired from training. Returning from a Newbury meeting in August 1969, he was severely injured in a car crash. He never recovered and died at the age of seventy one in Chichester Hospital the following month.

*   *   *

The third volume of the autobiography of John Hislop, *Hardly a Jockey* was published by Marlborough Books early in 1993. It covers the immediate post-war years in which the author was Champion Amateur Jockey on the flat for eleven consecutive seasons from 1946 until 1956, with the remarkably consistent record of having ridden eighty seven winners and fifty three placed horses from 177 mounts. He also continued riding over fences and hurdles during the first six years following his return from the war. Among the most notable of the eighteen races that John won from exactly 100 rides were the Coronation Hurdle on Coubrador at Liverpool in 1949, easily beating horses ridden by professionals, Glen Kelly and the great Martin Molony, while the previous season he had won the Golden Miller Chase on Cloncarrig, trained by Tom Masson for Sir Alan Gordon-Smith, with the Grand National winners Freebooter and Lovely Cottage among the beaten horses. In addition John Hislop was third in the Grand National of 1947 on Kami. Besides recounting his experiences in the saddle, he gives fascinating *vignettes* of the likes of George Todd and other leading racing professionals of that era, all of whom he knew well.

The first two volumes of John Hislop's autobiography were *Far From a Gentleman* (Michael Joseph, 1960) and *Anything But A Soldier* (Michael Joseph, 1965). The former contains one of the most hilarious descriptions of a race in the whole literature of the Turf, the event in question culminating with the appearance of the author and the late Staff Ingham in front of a decidedly unsympathetic panel of stewards at Hawthorn Hill.

Other books written by John Hislop include *The Turf* (Collins 1948), *Steeplechasing* (Hutchinson, 1951), *Breeding for Racing* (Secker &

142

Warburg, 1976, revised edition from the Kingswood Press, 1992). In collaboration with the late Major David Swannell, for many years senior Jockey Club handicapper, he edited *The Faber Book of The Turf,* an anthology of racing literature, first published in 1990, and re-issued as a paperback in 1992.

John Hislop is, of course, also the author of *The Brigadier* (Secker & Warburg, 1973), the story of the racing career of the great horse he bred and raced in partnership with his wife. The winner of seventeen of his eighteen races, including the Two Thousand Guineas, the King George VI and Queen Elizabeth Stakes and the Champion Stakes twice, Brigadier Gerard was by Queen's Hussar out of La Paiva, who can be traced back in the female line to that great mare Pretty Polly, who won the One Thousand Guineas, the Oaks and St. Leger of 1904 while trained by Peter Purcell Gilpin in the Clarehaven Stable at Newmarket.

*　　*　　*

John Hislop was born at Quetta in Baluchistan on 12th December 1911, the son of an officer in the 35th Scinde Horse. He was educated at Wellington College and The Royal Military College, Sandhurst. While assistant to Victor Gilpin, son of Peter Purcell Gilpin, first at Clarehaven, then at Michel Grove, Sussex, he became a leading amateur rider both on the flat and over fences. After distinguished service in the Sussex Yeomanry and then the Special Air Service, and being awarded the Military Cross during the war, he achieved a high reputation as a journalist, as well as resuming his riding career. In addition to being Editor of *The British Racehorse,* he was racing correspondent to *The Observer.*

In 1971 John Hislop was elected to The Jockey Club. He lives at Exning, near Newmarket.

£320,000 ON A PONY'S NOSE

(A Bet on a 1939 Pony Race)

Introduction by R.O. : During the years immediately preceding the outbreak of the Second World War in 1939, pony racing became an increasingly popular medium of betting. At the meetings at Northolt Park, as well as at Hawthorn Hill, Portsmouth Park and Shirley Park, the market was strong enough to accommodate some of the biggest punters of the era.

The races were confined to thoroughbreds, two-year-olds of no more than 14.3 hands and older horses 15 hands, and were run under the jurisdiction of the Pony Turf Club. As that body was in reciprocal agreement with the Jockey Club, people participating in pony racing were in no danger of being declared Disqualified Persons. Moreover a number of trainers and jockeys successfully made the transition from the ponies to racing under Jockey Club Rules. Tommy Carey rode the 1943 Derby winner Straight Deal, while Bill Wightman, doyen of the trainers of the present day, commenced his career with a successful spell of handling ponies.

*   *   *

Geoffrey Hamlyn recalls the betting at Northolt Park to the West of London. The facilities of the course were superior to those on almost any other course in the country.

*   *   *

Everybody who ever went racing at Northolt Park before the Second World War, agreed that it was thirty years before its time.

It was first with the racecourse commentary - Leonard Jayne did it admirably for several hundred races before war broke out in 1939 - and it was the first racecourse to stage evening racing every Wednesday during the summer months between 1934 and 1939 - *not* Hamilton

145

Park in 1947 as is usually stated in the Press. Believe it or not, some Members even turned up in evening dress.

Another innovation was the large electrical timing clock standing in full view of the Members and Tattersalls' stands, the only one at that time on any English racecourse. But most important of all was the introduction of Stipendiary Stewards, many years before Stewards Secretaries became the norm on Jockey Club courses. The "stipes" had already been operating in various parts of the then British Empire. One such was Claud Kirkwood, who was appointed as the general overseer of betting. He was empowered to organise all the betting facilities in the various rings, and to deal with disputes, defaulters, etc. He did a magnificent job in this respect, and subsequently joined Ladbrokes, where he was a member of the staff for the best part of twenty years.

The market in Tattersalls was as strong as that at many of the minor meetings. I can remember the Members Ring as though it was yesterday. Archie Cohen was next to the gate and with his partner 'Wag' Wagstaff, was generally regarded as leader of the ring. Next to him came Sol Goldhill, a prominent bookmaker-owner-breeder from Australia, who returned there on the outbreak of war. Then came Ernie Hunter Simmonds, father of Michael, the present rep of Heathowns Ltd., since the deaths of his father and his uncle, Charlie Simmonds. William Hill occupied the next pitch from 1934 onwards, after betting on the boards in partnership with 'Buck' Carr for a short time previously. By 1939, he had become almost the strongest of the layers, although of course, only a shadow of what he was to become. Finally there was a bookmaker called Spinks, who bet under the standard of Alfred Bros..

The board bookmakers were in two lines facing each other. It was perhaps no coincidence that the two on the end pitches were Billy Chandler, uncle of the present Victor who was tragically killed in an accident at Salisbury in 1945, and the firm of Percy and Warwick Thompson. Percy bet there chiefly at evening meetings, but was always represented. Both would lay a £1,000 bet.

The Blower and Exchange Telegraph were always in attendance and transacted a fair amount of business during most afternoons. Professional backers were in rather short supply, although a few did turn up on otherwise blank Mondays. The market was chiefly shaped by owners and trainers, and bookmakers compiled their prices in accordance with what they considered the connections' confidence in their runners. I do not pretend to remember a great deal about the activities of various stables, although once the partnership of Pat Donoghue as trainer and Tommy Carey as jockey became established, they usually started favourite, especially in the more important races.

Pat was not known to wager extensively, but Carey's activities as a punter were common knowledge. They eventually led to his downfall some fifteen years later, a major tragedy for so gifted a rider, and later a successful trainer. He had a run of good fortune in the early fifties and one prominent layer in the South told me that Carey had won over £100,000 (£1,300,000) off him alone one year. This was a period when it was a known fact that certain jockeys backed horses, some of them heavily.

There was a story at Northolt, probably apocryphal, that a winner of an important race there ran a furlong or so beyond the winning post (which it was perfectly possible to do, as it was a park in every sense of the word), and had his weights re-adjusted in the saddle cloth prior to weighing in. The story did not explain how the weights left the saddle cloth after the weigh-out, but the fable was widely believed.

Apart from *The Sporting Life* and *The Sporting Chronicle,* Northolt Park received quite a lot of publicity in the National Press, particularly in *The Daily Express* from Geoffrey Gilbey, whose racing column was very widely read throughout the country. Geoffrey owned a number of ponies, and won the valuable Metropolitan Plate (the pony equivalent of the Two Thousand Guineas) in 1934 with Grand Slam, the champion two-year-old of the previous year. Grand Slam won numerous other races, both for Gilbey and my father-in-law, Mr. F.J. Lawes, who also owned one of the best sprinters under Pony Turf Club Rules, the mare Holt. Geoffrey Gilbey attended most meetings, except when he had to be at important Jockey Club races and was by far the keenest member of the National press. Meyrick Good, 'Man on the Spot' on *The Sporting Life* for sixty years, came when he could, and won races with his filly Glanconia.

Geoffrey Gilbey was also instrumental in introducing Leonard Jayne and the trainer Bill Wightman to Northolt. Bill, now seventy-eight, is the senior trainer under both Jockey Club and National Hunt Rules.

The whole Northolt Park operation was master-minded by the late W.A. Read. He was a most dynamic man, and was Vice Chairman of the Northolt Park Racecourse Company. Of medium height, with snow white hair, he was always impeccably turned out in dark, double breasted suits and a black Homburg hat. Born in New Zealand, he had vast administrative experience of racing in the U.S.A., Australia, Canada and Jamaica, and got his initiation into pony racing in the first named country. He was given *carte blanche* to create a totally different type of racing and racecourse amenities and very successfully he did it too. He got on well with everybody, especially the bookmakers, and was responsible for the appointment of Claud Kirkwood as Stipendiary Steward in charge of betting.

As I have already written, during the years 1933 to 1937, wagering was on a fairly modest scale . All that changed with the arrival of the Honourable Miss Dorothy Paget in the summer of 1937. Things were fairly quiet at first, although her first runner, Crumb, was a winner after scoring in a moderate race at Leicester. If my memory is correct, Crumb started at 9 - 4 on. Miss Paget had a number of winners in 1938, all trained by Pat Donoghue and ridden by Tommy Carey, but it was in 1939 that she really hit the jackpot. She owned probably the best pony ever to run at Northolt, Scottish Rifle, a son of the 1931 Derby winner, Cameronian. Her Secretaries usually shared out her mammoth wagers between Ernie Hunter Simmonds, William Hill and Billy Chandler, but to the best of my knowledge, they gave Hill £10,000 (£320,000) to put on Scottish Rifle for the Metropolitan Plate. As the horse had won the Champion Two Year Old Plate at 8 - 1 on the previous autumn, he looked something to bet on. He started at 10 - 1 on and won easily. He was always odds on for the Northolt Derby that year and easily landed the double at the relatively generous odds of 2 - 1 on. On the outbreak of war, Scottish Rifle was exported to Malaya, where he was trained for a while by Michael Silley, who was the Northern representative of *Raceform* for a number of years after the war. He returned to England at the end of 1945, after being a prisoner of the Japanese for four years. Scottish Rifle was also captured and presumably sent to Japan to augment their bloodstock industry.

I was responsible for returning Starting Prices at Northolt from March 1933 until September, 1939 as well as all the other pony racing activities such as runners and jockeys, full detailed return, plus of course selections for *The Sporting Life*. It was only with the arrival of Dorothy Paget that returning the SP became difficult, but thanks to Claud Kirkwood and the cooperation of most of the bookmakers, a *modus vivendi* was arrived at and remained until the track closed down the weekend France fell in June 1940.

It is a tragedy that the course was never allowed to re-open after the war. The ten boom years enjoyed by racing in general would have brought massive crowds to the South Harrow track and solved all their financial difficulties - they were in the hands of the Official Receiver for two years before the outbreak of hostilities. One member of the Labour controlled Council was alleged to have said that Northolt would only open over his dead body. Nye Bevan, Minister of Health in the Attlee Government endorsed this decision, on the grounds that the land was required for building. But as far as I know, not a brick was laid there until Harold Macmillan became Minister of Housing in Winston Churchill's last Government.

*   *   *

Conclusion by R.O.: Memories of some of the less instantly likeable members of the recently dissolved Reichstag were revived in late 1945, when the Stewards of the Pony Turf Club and the Directors of Northolt Park read in a Sunday newspaper that Mr. James Hudson, the little known Socialist Member of Parliament for Ealing West, had informed Ealing Council that he had obtained from his Right Honourable Friend Mr. Lewis Silkin, the Minister for Town and Country Planning, permission for some 1,000 houses to be built on the racecourse. The right of appeal to the Minister of Health, Mr Aneurin Bevan, existed, but seemed of little more use than asking the devil to rebuke sin. All the same it was the only available procedure and would have to be followed if there was to be any hope at all of saving Northolt Park for racing.

By way of a preliminary skirmish, Mr. Edward Mason, Senior Steward of the Pony Turf Club, wrote to the Minister. Among several telling points that he made was that "...racing at Northolt Park was conducted on the best possible lines strictly and cleanly. Racegoers enjoyed sport under conditions unrivalled in Great Britain; the stands and other appointments of the course are the finest in the country; the standards of the sport are exceptionally high and the admission charges are reasonable. Here was the perfect racecourse for the working man, for the man of moderate means and for women. Saturday afternoons and annual evening charity meetings (unique gatherings in Great Britain) were widely appreciated by people from all over London and the Home Counties." However it was all to no avail.

A two-day Public Inquiry into the desirability of building on Northolt Park opened at Ealing Town Hall on 7th May, 1946. Mr. Scott Henderson K.C., for the racecourse authorities, quickly established that Northolt was an important open space, of exceptional recreational value. On the other hand, the Down Barns, which offered Ealing Council an alternative building site, was low-grade agricultural land fit for nothing more than growing poor quality hay. Moreover the land on the Down Barns would cost £600 an acre, whereas the compulsory purchase of Northolt Park would entail the ratepayer paying £1,600 an acre.

Finally Mr. Scott Henderson asked Mr. C.W. Seddon, Ealing Borough Councils' Surveyor "Have you heard Mr. Silkin say 'Plan on Broad Lines, and never mind the cost'?"

The official confirmed that such was the case.

All arguments, however cogent, persuasive or logical, could make no impression on the Ministry of Health's inspector Mr. H.H. Jewell. He ruled that Ealing Council should be able to compulsorily purchase the 150 acres of Northolt Park for the construction of a housing estate, despite the alternative offered by the Barn Downs, acquisition of which would deprive nobody of leisure or livelihood.

It was a tragedy. "The Newmarket of Pony Racing" was wiped off the map by the unsavoury alliance of insensitive bureaucrats and kill-joy politicians, just when its future was looking brighter than it had done for many years. By 1945 Northolt Park, where meetings had been discontinued on the outbreak of war, was in serious financial trouble and in the hands of the Official receiver, but Mr. Neal Christey had offered to buy it for £240,000 and revive the racing, if he could receive assurance from Ealing Council that there would be no compulsory purchase. The closure of Northolt Park was the harbinger of the end. Edward Mason, of Pophole Farm, Liss in Hampshire, who had tried so hard to save the London course, in his capacity of Senior Steward, died after a long illness in 1948. Shortly afterwards Pony Racing was abandoned. Northolt Park, the flagship of the sport, was an exceptionally fine and progressive course, by any standards. Not only was it the course that introduced evening racing, as mentioned by Geoffrey Hamlyn, but it was the first to stage meetings in aid of charity, now a commonplace feature of racing under Jockey Club rules, as intimated by Edward Mason in his letter to the Minister of Health.

*　　*　　*

Returning the starting prices at Northolt Park was one of the many facets of a distinguished career, which culminated in *Geoffrey Hamlyn* becoming Senior Starting Price Reporter of *The Sporting Life.* An account of his fascinating experiences in the ring, and the high betting men and women on both sides of the rails,with whom he has been closely acquainted over a period of six decades, will be found in his autobiography *My Sixty Years in The Ring,* to be published by Marlborough Books in 1994.

Born in 1910, Geoffrey Hamlyn was educated at Dulwich College. On leaving School in 1928, without any intention of making a career in racing, he worked in a bank in Berkeley Street from 9 a.m to 7 p.m. for 37s.6d.(£1.37½p) a week, and was bored stiff. After three months he left to work for his father, who published a successful weekly racing paper called *Sporting Chat.* On New Year's Eve 1932 he joined *The Sporting Life.* He received Lord Derby's Award for The Journalist of the Year in 1969, retired in 1975, and is now Public Relations Officer to Victor Chandler, the rails bookmaker.

John McCririck refers to him as "The oldest man in the World", which is not quite correct, but it is true that he is one of the most respected and loved personalities on British racecourses. The running of the Geoffrey Hamlyn Handicap at Kempton Park each September speaks for the esteem in which he is held.

THE FRANCASAL FIASCO

(A Ringer at Bath in 1953)

Introduction by R.O: A festival atmosphere pervaded Britain throughout the summer of 1953. The Queen was crowned on 2nd June and four days later the newly knighted Sir Gordon Richards finally achieved the ambition of a lifetime by riding the winner of the Derby, his mount Pinza, having been heavily backed by the public.

The following month a group of individuals, of very much less exemplary character than the Champion Jockey, began to move to centre stage after a horse running in the name of Francasal won a very small race at Bath. As a result of the energetic investigation undertaken by Scotland Yard, working in close collaboration with the Jockey Club's Security Services, five men were brought to the dock of the Old Bailey in March 1954. All pleaded not guilty to conspiring to cheat and defraud the Bath Racecourse Company by falsely representing that a horse running in the two o'clock race at Bath on July 16, 1953, in the name of Francasal, was, in fact, Santa Amaro; and conspiring to win money by similar false pretences.

The defendants were Henry George Kateley, 42, bookmaker, of Queen Street, Maidenhead, Berkshire. Victor Robert Colquhoun Dill, 56, dealer, of Jubilee Place, Chelsea SW. William Maurice Williams, 47, builder's decorator of Malden Road, Kentish Town N.W. Gomer Charles, 46, turf accountant of Park Place, Cardiff and William Rook, 57, engineer, of Taplow Common Road, Burnham, Buckinghamshire.

*   *   *

Jack Millan tells the story of how almost unbelievable incompetence and folly led to the exposure of a ringer.

*   *   *

When the bookmakers manage to avoid paying out over a winner, public sympathy is almost invariably with the frustrated punters. But few felt sorry for the men who almost separated the layers from a fortune on the result of the Spa Selling Plate at Bath on July 16, 1953. They simply did not deserve to collect.

It was bad enough that the operation was crooked from start to finish. On top of that, they were incredibly clumsy. The rat would not have been smelled any earlier had they dabbed cologne behind his ears and sent him round to William Hill's office with the betting instructions in a pouch tied round his neck.

In bookmaking offices round Britain, wagers totalling more than £6,000 were placed by telephone at starting price on a little known runner in the humble Bath curtain-raiser, a two-year-old called Francasal.

With William Gilchrist in the saddle, this dark horse never gave his supporters the slightest anxiety. In front after the first of the six furlongs, he was clearly in command well before the finish and came home a length-and-a-half clear.

But, although odds of 10-1 were returned, the only recorded pay-out was £175 to an inspired racecourse guesser who got his pony on too soon.

The £6,000 which was known to have been placed at S.P would have won £780,000 in today's money.

Long before the off-course gamblers' cheques were due to be sent out, the bookmakers' union, the National Sporting League, instructed its members to withhold payment at least until knavery had been ruled out. And, as knavery was in fact quickly established, those cheques remained unwritten. But why was not a penny of a sum approximating to £78,000 at today's values sent through to the Bath betting ring to reduce the offices' liabilities of £780,000?

The horse known as Francasal opened at 6-1 in the betting and drifted to tens in the face of a course gamble on a rival called Eastern Magic, from the same opening odds down to 6-4. Had even half the office money got to the track, it would not have been Eastern Magic who went off hot favourite, and the starting price firms would not have been facing the prospect of paying out about three quarters of a million pounds in today's money.

The course bookmakers were never alerted to the Francasal gamble because the normal channel of communication was blocked at the crucial moment.

154

This was not a consequence, as many believed at the time, of an act of God in the shape of a thunderstorm which raged over Bath shortly after midday.

It was the act of Rhondda Valley scrap metal dealer called Leonard Phillips. Half-an-hour before the tapes were raised on the Spa Selling Plate, he drove up Lansdown Hill, less than a mile from Bath racecourse, in a red Bedford truck bearing a passing resemblance to a Post Office van. Near the top he got out and, using an extension ladder steadied by an accomplice, he scaled a telegraph pole and sheared the lead covered cable with a blow lamp. The effect of this was to isolate Bath racecourse from the rest of the world.

The racing press, unable to make direct contact with their Fleet Street headquarters, set up a taxi shuttle service to a public telephone box two miles away. But that link was not established until after racing began, and even then it was unavailable to bookmakers outside Bath attempting to communicate with colleagues on the spot.

Imagine the frustration felt by men generally able to knock the market into any shape that suits them. Imagine the tension in the offices during the extra-long wait for the result. And when it came, ringing like a Lutine Bell, imagine the anguish.

No wonder William Hill, who was still at that time betting on the rails, grasped eagerly at the lifebelt cast by the news that the telephone cable had been severed by illegal means. Britain's biggest bookmaker, facing the heaviest liabilities over the Francasal gamble, was the first to ask the National Sporting League for a ruling.

But Hill and the NSL were not the prime movers in the investigations which foiled the coup and culminated in five men going to prison.

The Stewards of the Jockey Club have often been accused of dragging their feet. But, less than twenty four hours after the Bath seller had been run, a meeting chaired by the Duke of Norfolk led to the head of the Club's security division, Colonel Neville Blair, speeding to Scotland Yard with vital information for Chief Superintendent Reginald Spooner, and the two did not hang about either.

Within three weeks, Leonard Phillips had been charged with "cutting a cable". And, six weeks later, he was imprisoned for three months after admitting he had done the job for just £35.

The floodgates were by then wide open. On the day of Phillips' conviction, five men were charged with "conspiracy to defraud Bath racecourse", and during their ten-day hearing from October 7th, at which evidence came from 147 witnesses, the whole tale unfolded.

It began across the Channel a little earlier the same year, when Maurice Williams, a bookmaker who lived in Kentish Town in London purchased two two-year-old bay colts from a French trainer named Maurice Wallon.

Williams paid £820 for Francasal, who had raced six times and been placed once, and £2,000 for Santa Amaro, whose form was clearly superior. Both horses were sent to Percy Bailey's Epsom stables, and it was from there that both were boxed up to go racing on July 16th, Francasal to Bath and Santa Amaro to Newmarket - or so Bailey believed.

In fact, it was Santa Amaro, who had worked much the better of the two in a preparatory gallop, who raced in Francasal's name at Bath, while the real Francasal, pretending to be Santa Amaro, was in a Stevenage lay-by following the reported breakdown of his horsebox on the A1.

Why the plotters bothered with this refinement is not clear. Indeed, when it was learned that they had telephoned Newmarket with the information that Santa Amaro had been unavoidably delayed, it simply added to the suspicions raised by the crude method employed to prevent news of the betting activity from reaching Bath.

Overnight declaration of runners was not required in those days. When an entry was not declared forty five minutes before the scheduled start, no questions were asked.

Anyway, during the half-hour between Bath racecourse being made *incommunicado* and "Francasal" finishing clear at the end of his only race in Britain, bookmakers all over the country were inundated with bets from smaller firms with hedging accounts which had been largely inactive since being opened months before.

Among Maurice Williams' interests was a Hampstead Turf Accounting business trading under the name J. Davidson & Co.. It was managed for him by a man calling himself Robert Colquhoun, and it was from this source that more than half the gamble was launched.

But a further £2,500 in bets emanated from accounts held by two more bookmakers, Gomer Charles of Cardiff and Harry George Kateley, junior, of Maidenhead, who traded in the West End of London.

Williams, Charles, Kateley, Colquhoun (under his real name, Colonel Victor Robert Dill) and one other were the men charged with the conspiracy. And, although the jury failed to agree when the five stood in the dock between January 12th and February 2nd, 1954, the first four named were all found guilty at the twenty three day retrial which ended on March 17th.

A link with Phillips and his blow torch had already been provided. Further evidence, from the French trainer, from the farrier who fitted the Bath winner's racing plates, from the horsebox drivers and from a vet all served to convince the jury that the horse was a ringer and that the connections were all fully aware of the fact.

Kateley was sentenced to gaol for three years, Charles and Williams to two apiece, Dill to nine months.

What of Francasal and Santa Amaro?

Within days of the attempted coup, police found them hidden near Reading, and, mindful that they were evidence liable to be tampered with, had them billeted under guard for almost a year with the Epsom vet, George Forbes.

But when the trial was over they did return to active life. They were warned off the Turf. But Francasal, sold for 160 guineas, developed into a useful polo pony, while Santa Amaro, who fetched 400 guineas, went on to a career in the show-ring.

*   *   *

Conclusion by R.O.: William Rook was acquitted. For some five years he had grazed horses with Mr. A.J. Layton at Cabbage Hill Farm, Binfield, Berkshire. Santa Amaro and Francasal were also at Cabbage Hill Farm, although not simultaneously, during the first seven months of 1953; one arriving in May, and the other on 18th July. At the second trial the court was told that Rook made no attempt to pretend they were the same horse. Margaret Layton testified that she had heard her father asking if the first horse was the same animal as the second, and Rook replying, "No".

In the course of the case, Colonel Victor Dill, who managed Maurice Williams' Hampstead credit office, was rightly described "as a retired regular army officer, an educated man", by reason of his having attended both Eton and the Royal Military College. Less complimentary remarks were made about the other occupants of the dock.

Mr. James Burge, who represented Gomer Charles, did not necessarily help his client when he opened the defence by telling the jury. "You really have got to the bottom of the barrel now". The story of Gomer Charles, who missed much of the trial on account of a bout of influenza, which left a patch on his lungs, is really rather sad.

For many years he had been a well respected bookmaker, in business in a big way in South Wales, until making the acquaintance of Harry Kateley, also a bookmaker and father of his co-defendant. Through the younger Kateley, he met Maurice Williams and Victor Dill. About ten years after completing his sentence, Gomer Charles was murdered on his own doorstep in Cardiff, by two young thieves.

Francasal ran in the name of Maurice Williams, who worked as a builder's decorator for £3 a week, when he was not buying horses for £2,000 in France. He did not trouble the Inland Revenue with an application for assessment, but was supplied with one on the opening of the first trial.

"He is one of those characters", his counsel Mr. F.H. Lawton, told the jury, "you have heard of, who go around with huge wads of five pound notes on them. What he does is to carry large sums of money on him, and always has an inside pocket made in his waistcoat, and another at the top of his trousers to make it as difficult as possible for pickpockets.

He lives with his sister in Kentish Town. She runs a small builders merchants' business. He is unmarried and devoted to his sister. He helps her in the business, and she pays him £3 a week. In his spare time he goes racing and betting.

He is a roughish diamond. Dill has described him as a shy man. But I should say he is self-conscious about the fact he lacks the social graces. That is very understandable, and not without its importance in this case. He keeps in the background."

Counsel said it might be asked, for instance, why Williams was not at Bath to see his horse run, and answered by way of a rhetorical question.

"What is he going to do if the Duke of Norfolk speaks to him?"

"Why the Duke of Norfolk should be dragged into it, I cannot imagine", interjected Mr. Justice Byrne.

Everybody agreed the Duke of Norfolk did not come into it. All the same Maurice Williams' admirable modesty stood him in no good stead on that occasion.

Among the jockeys whose mounts trailed in behind Francasal/Santa Amaro in that infamous race at Bath forty years ago, were Lester Piggott, Joe Mercer and Jimmy Lindley.

When the police auctioned the real Francasal at Epsom, that extremely moderate individual was bought by David Methven, a retired cavalry officer who had had steeplechasers in training with Bay Powell at Aldbourne before the war. David Methven's nephew Keith Gillies, the well known London solicitor, has had a number of useful horses, such as Tenochca, with Paul Cole over the last twenty years.

*   *   *

Jack Millan began his career as a general sports sub-editor on *The Sporting Post* in Dundee in 1953. In 1956 he became assistant editor and columnist in *The Racehorse*, combining those duties with the editing of *The Winner* from 1964. In August 1974, he joined *The Daily Mail*, and wrote the Robin Goodfellow column for that paper until 1992, winning *The Sporting Life* naps table no fewer than four times. He has resumed his career as a freelance with great success, and lives at Epsom.

£500 TO £5 WILL DO TO START

(Snowy Parker and Pelican Star)

Introduction by R.O.: If ever a man could make a silk purse out of a sow's ear, that man was the former Epsom trainer Snowy Parker. He worked miracles with the most unlikely material, giving the bookmakers some very nasty surprises indeed.

Snowy Parker obtained his first experience of racing while watching greyhounds running at Monmore Green during his boyhood in Birmingham, with the result that the breeding and racing of the long dogs, with whom he obtained notable success at Wimbledon, became a lifelong hobby. At the age of fifteen he left home to go to Newmarket to be apprenticed to that versatile horseman Bill Halsey, who had been second in the Grand National on Barsac in 1900, before winning the Two Thousand Guineas on Handicapper the following year and the St. Leger on Woolwinder in 1907. After injuries sustained in a heavy fall had brought his career as a steeplechase jockey to an end, Snowy Parker became private trainer to the brewer J. Reid Walker at Shifnal, Shropshire, until opening his own stable, which was called Shifnal Cottage, at Epsom in 1940.

*   *   *

Michael Ford recalls how Snowy Parker shot a bolt from the blue, so far as the bookmakers were concerned, when he turned up at a flat fixture at Nottingham with a seven-year-old steeplechaser.

*   *   *

You will not find the name of Evan James Parker in the reference books as the trainer of any famous winners, but Snowy Parker was indubitably one of the cleverest stablemen of this century. The

161

legendary Stanley Wootton once said to him, "I have always regarded Fred Darling as the greatest trainer of the present time, but you run him very close." Snowy Parker never had more than about a dozen horses in his Shifnal Cottage stable on Burgh Heath Road, Epsom, but he knew absolutely everything there was to know about every one of them. At the same time he ensured that everybody else had access to only the bare minimum of information about them. He never talked to the press. Nobody kept a stable secret closer than Snowy. And when he bet, the bookmakers almost always had something to remember for many a long day.

One of the most unlikely candidates for a gamble that he ever produced was the steeplechaser Pelican Star, whom he saddled for the mile and five furlong Ratcliffe Maiden Handicap at Nottingham on 5th July, 1955. Pelican Star had originally been trained by Jack Pearce in the Richmond House Stable at Malton in Yorkshire. A brown son of The Pelican, Pelican Star was unplaced at York, Doncaster and Newcastle as a two-year-old, and then down the field again when only ninth of twelve in a seller at Pontefract, on his final appearance at that age in 1950.

Pelican Star did not run on the flat in 1951, and after having had him cut, Jack Pearce sent him hurdling. As a jumper, the horse proved a great deal more effective than on the flat. As well as winning at Catterick Bridge and Market Rasen, he was in the first four on eight other occasions from a dozen appearances. Put to fencing early as a four-year-old at the outset of the season of 1952, Pelican Star revealed the same consistency by winning two-mile handicap 'chases at Nottingham, Market Rasen, Southwell and Wetherby.

Missing the flat for the third consecutive season in 1953, Pelican Star obtained his last success for Jack Pearce when, ridden by his regular partner Percy Wigham, he beat Pearl's Choice by four lengths in a handicap 'chase over an extended two miles at Doncaster on 21st November, 1953. Pelican Star was not seen on the flat again in 1954, but in the course of the season, was sent to Snowy Parker at Epsom, while remaining the property of Miss E. M. Goddard.

Pelican Star obtained his first success for his new trainer when Ken Mullins rode him to win the Old Mill Handicap Chase at Lingfield in February 1955. On his final appearance of the season he was fourth to

162

the good class Greenogue at Towcester on 7th May. By that time Snowy had already come to appreciate the possibility of exploiting Pelican Star on the flat, something the bookmakers could never have anticipated, and had given the old horse a number of engagements, including the Periosteum Maiden Plate, to be run over a mile-and-a-quarter at Folkestone on 21st June. Making a long delayed return to the flat in that event, Pelican Star was out with the washing amongst the "20/1 others" in a field of sixteen and ridden by the Australian Eddie Cracknell, finished in the middle of the field in eighth position.

Fifteen days later, Pelican Star reappeared among the ten runners for the Ratcliffe Handicap at Nottingham, where that good Epsom lightweight Tommy Carter was in the saddle. So far as the bookmakers, and everybody else unconnected with the stable were concerned, he was just a seven-year-old steeplechaser, a maiden on the flat, who had not run under Jockey Club rules for five years, apart from a recent and unremarkable performance at Folkestone. It seemed impossible to fancy him to beat the favourite Whitehall Bloom, ridden by Ken Gethin and a winner over the course and distance four weeks earlier, or Eph Smith's mount, Brasoss who had landed a hot seller at Kempton Park for Les Hall's gambling stable last time out. Nobody seems to have thought that some residual speed in Pelican Star might have been sharpened up by his outing at Folkestone, or that the obvious stamina of the jumper would be given greater play over the extra three furlongs at Nottingham.

As the betting on the Ratcliffe Handicap opened at the evening meeting at Nottingham in that sweltering summer of 1955, one bookmaker contemptuously offered 100-1 against the Epsom steeplechaser, and found himself laying £500 to a fiver. More money for Pelican Star trickled into the ring, and he eventually started at 100-7. There was, however, another outsider being quietly backed for that little handicap worth £264 almost exactly less than half the two-year-old seller immediately preceding it. This was the four-year-old Warm Spring, trained by his owner Mr. F. Clark at Gerwyn Hall near Wrexham in North Wales, and ridden by the 5 lbs. claiming apprentice Peter Robinson, father of that fine rider of the present time Philip Robinson.

In the early exchanges, Warm Spring appeared on the boards with 50 - 1 against her name, and a bet of £1,000 to £20 was very quickly struck. Sustained support for Warm Spring, a daughter of the 1937 Derby winner Mid-day Sun, followed at all rates down to her starting price of 10 - 1. Whitehall Bloom, trained by Harold Wallington senior at Epsom, headed the market at no more than 5 - 4, but a number of bookmakers had heavy liabilities over two of the outsiders.

As the tapes rose, Whitehall Bloom took up a prominent position, with Pelican Star well in touch with the leaders in the early stages. After only five furlongs, Pelican Star went to the front, and led into the straight from Shining Guinea, ridden by Davy Jones. Once in line for home, Warm Spring began to make relentless progress until taking the lead inside the final furlong. Refusing to accept defeat twenty five year old Tommy Carter, who had been taught his trade by George Todd, asked the veteran for a renewed effort, and with Pelican Star responding with the utmost courage, he got up on the line to force a dead heat with the filly.

The gamble on the steeplechaser, stepping outside his milieu, had not entirely come off, but half a loaf was better than none. The backers of Pelican Star still had plenty to come, and the bookmakers nothing to laugh about.

Pelican Star ran twice more that season, being unplaced at Folkestone and second to Galloway Lad on returning to Nottingham in August, before continuing his jumping career. During the season of 1955/6 he won a two-and-a-half-mile hurdle at Nottingham, and was only out of the first four twice in fourteen outings. After completing a treble at Fontwell, Plumpton and Hurst Park the following season, he was sold to a patron of Roy Whiston's Shropshire stable, for whom he won at Uttoxeter in May 1958, and again on his final appearance in public when Tim Brookshaw rode him to win a two-mile chase at Newton Abbot on 3rd September, 1958.

Tough, versatile and consistent, Pelican Star must have been easy to train as a jumper, but it was real brilliance to bring off a coup with him as a seven-year-old maiden on the flat - even if the spoils did have to be shared.

*   *   *

Conclusion by R.O.: When I had the pleasure of interviewing Snowy Parker for *The Sporting Life* on the occasion of his ninetieth birthday on 6th February, 1990, the racing world that he knew had long vanished. In his day, trainers, jockeys and lads would never give information about horses to the press, let alone discuss their prospects or possible programmes on television for dissemination to millions of viewers. Not only was it a breach of confidence in that era before the betting levy, but a gross dereliction of duty owed to the owners who paid the training fees. A stable secret had to be exactly that, and was far too valuable a commodity to be shared. Moreover with all too many races worth £207 or as little £138, trainers did not get fat on their percentages of prize money, and had to rely on successful betting for their incomes, so that every possible measure to protect the price had to be taken.

Another facet of modern racing that Snowy Parker found incomprehensible was the stable with 100 horses, or an even greater number in it, and people not training their own horses any more. He looked back to the times when the likes of Stanley Wootton and Herbert Blagrave generally owned all the horses in their yards, while for his own part he never had more than fourteen horses in his stable. At that time he owned them all himself, and they won thirty four races during the course of the season.

Long before it had earned official censure, Snowy Parker was deploring the prolific use of the whip. He would never allow a horse to be knocked about on the course or in his box. He once bought a gelding called Good View for £400 from Atty Persse, only to find the animal was savage, and often practically uncontrollable. All the same, Snowy Parker would never allow him to be hit. Gradually Good View responded to kindness, and eventually won the Chichester Handicap at Goodwood as a twelve-year-old. Snowy Parker's horses may never have had a great deal of class, but they received the very best of attention, and were placed with uncanny skill.

When he retired in 1968 Snowy Parker was taken aback by one of the lads saying, "You weren't a trainer" and then adding, after a pause: "You were a genius." Anyone who knew him, or had even a passing knowledge of his achievements, would have agreed with that. Snowy Parker may have held his cards close to his chest, but he always played fair. Even the bookmakers knew that.

*　　*　　*

Michael Ford has contributed to a wide variety of newspapers, magazines and other publications. He lives in Surrey, not so very many miles from Epsom, where Snowy Parker trained with such great success.

A SICK RELATION

(Barney Curley's 1975 Coup at Bellewstown)

Introduction by R.O: A highly developed sense of of moral values, together with rigid observation of etiquette, has not prevented Barney Curley from becoming one of the most controversial personalities on the racing scene in the British Isles. Long before his arrival in England, to train his own horses in the Harraton Court Stables at Exning, near Newmarket, Mr. Curley had cut his teeth by taking some very large bites out of the flesh of the bookmakers at home in Ireland.

*   *   *

Sean Magee recalls the ingenuity with which Barney Curley pulled off his great coup at the little Irish meeting at Bellewstown, back in June 1975.

*   *   *

You need a pretty large-scale map of Ireland to find Bellewstown. If you're driving there from Dublin, taking the N1 towards Belfast, you must keep your eyes peeled for the sign off to the left about twenty-five miles north of the capital, after Balbriggan and a little before Drogheda. Make that turn and climb through the winding lanes for a few miles, following your instinct as much as your nose, and you arrive at the racecourse.

The views from the edge of the track, perched high on a hill beside the small village with its two pubs - the Bellewstown Inn and the Cozy Bar - are spectacular, with the Mountains of Mourne in the distance, and closer to hand the same stretch of coastline on which is held, one day a year at Laytown, Europe's only official horse racing along the beach.

If Irish racegoers referred to their humbler tracks by the English term 'gaffs', Bellewstown would certainly come into that category. One of the oldest Irish racecourses, it now stages just one three-day meeting each year, and recent innovations include a roof on each of its two stands and a running rail - the course did well enough without one until the constant risk of the runners colliding with picnic parties made its installation a necessity.

Bellewstown does not often hit the headlines, but on 25 June 1975 a five-year-old brown gelding named Yellow Sam put the track firmly into the chronicles of the great betting coups when landing the Mount Hanover Handicap Hurdle for amateur riders.

That Yellow Sam raced in the colours of Mrs. B.J. Curley would be enough nowadays to alert followers of racing to the possibility that a touch was being attempted, as Mrs. Curley's husband has become a legend of the betting ring. Clad in camel coat with an ample fedora covering his shaven head, Barney Curley is a familiar sight stalking around the bookmakers at the major meetings like some panther on the prowl, and his reputation as a professional gambler is huge, with the £250,000 he reportedly won on Reference Point's Derby, or the £200,000 from Assultan (trained by Curley himself) in a handicap hurdle at Ascot in November 1988 lodged in the annals of the great winning bets.

At the root of the mystique of Barney Curley's persona is his having trained at St Mungret's College in County Limerick to become a Jesuit priest - and his rejection of the religious life in favour of one as a professional gambler is viewed as a spectacular instance of switching from God to Mammon. Any such notion is too simplistic, of course, and there is at the root of Curley's attitude to his latter calling a morality which underpinned his first. He gave a revealing insight into his moral position to the Irish journalist Raymond Smith for the book *The High Rollers of the Turf:*

"In battling to survive you have to be careful not to do anything that is morally wrong. What I mean by morally wrong is - to quote you the ultimate example - owning all five runners in a five-horse race, then stopping the four seen to have any chance and fixing it to win with the complete outsider.

It's morally wrong also if you can manage to stop the clock and you lay a bet on the 3 o'clock race when the bookmaker thinks it's 2.55 and you already know the result. That's stealing money from the bookmaker. Yes, daylight robbery is morally wrong and you have to answer for it.

It's morally wrong also if you fix races by squaring jockeys to do what is totally out of bounds. Again you have to answer for that."

On the other hand, it's quite within the bounds of any reasonable punter's moral code to land a legitimate touch by exploiting the mechanics of the betting business and the circumstances applying at any particular race meeting, and the Yellow Sam coup at Bellewstown was a beautiful example of a simple starting price coup.

The theory is straightforward enough. Lay out a horse for a particular race, do not overstrain it to show its top form in the races leading up to that event, and take advantage of the resulting long price in the targeted race by spreading bets in small amounts around a wide range of off-course betting shops. The individual small wagers will not attract attention at first, and the trick is to prevent that off-course money being put into the on-course market and depressing the starting price. An insignificant race at a small track is the ideal medium, as this will attract little outside interest.

The usual means by which off-course money reaches the on-course market is by the 'blower' system, a telephone connection to the course. At the core of the famous Gay Future sting at Cartmel in August 1984 was the perpetrators' knowledge that there would be no blower to that minor track on a busy Bank Holiday, though to make assurance doubly sure the plan included such contingencies as a switch of horses, the elaborate charade of other horses from the same stable being entered at other meetings but failing to get to their destinations (thus making doubles and trebles on the three horses into single bets), and the extra-nice touch of rubbing soap flakes into Gay Future's neck before he entered the parade ring to make it appear that he was in a lather of over-excitement.

The Yellow Sam coup, which took place less than a year after the Gay Future, was much simpler.

The gelding was trained for Mrs. Maureen Curley at The Curragh by Liam Brennan - not one of the big names of Irish training - and before the Bellewstown race had shown little worthwhile form. In 1974 his best placing from five races was eighth. (In one of those outings, interestingly, he was ridden by top amateur jockey Tim Jones, some two months after Jones had partnered Gay Future to victory in the

Cartmel race.) Yellow Sam had run three times in 1975 before his date with destiny: ninth at Limerick and nineteenth at Mallow in March, and twenty-second at Navan in May. In all he had run ten races in his life, and had never reached a place.

Given his form, the 20-1 against Yellow Sam in the Mount Hanover Handicap Hurdle did not seem excessively generous. In the 'upside down' handicap - like the present 'long handicap' system, but weighting horses from the worst up rather than from the best down - the gelding was allotted 10st. 6lb.. There were nine runners, and their riders included names who were already or were to become very familiar: Sam Morshead, Willie Mullins, Ted Walsh, John Fowler, and Mrs. Ann Ferris, who in 1984 would become the first lady to ride the winner of the Irish Grand National. Yellow Sam himself was ridden by Michael Furlong, later to be associated with that fine chaser Bannow Rambler, brought down by the fatal fall of Lanzarote when the subject of a major punt in the 1977 Cheltenham Gold Cup.

As Michael Furlong was steering Yellow Sam towards the $2\frac{1}{2}$-mile start on Bellewstown's gorse-lined circuit, Curley's men had already been in action in betting shops around the country, staking smallish bets - nothing more than £50 - on the gelding to win at starting price, and it was now that the particularly ingenious aspect of the coup came into effect. Once the off-course bookmakers began to realise their accumulated liabilities on the horse they would need to transfer much of the money they had taken into the on-course market, which would bring down the horse's odds. Their means of communicating with the on-course layers was by the single public telephone on the Bellewstown track (this was of course well before the days of mobile 'phones), and as chance would have it the off-course bookies just could not get through, as the line to the course was constantly busy.

This happy - for him - coincidence is explained by Barney Curley:

"There was this heavily built man, a tough sort of guy, who suddenly discovered that a close relation of his was seriously ill and he had to keep in constant touch with the hospital.

Once he had the 'phone in his hand he was not going to let go. He was broad enough in the beam not to permit anyone past him into the box."

Poor fellow: it must have been a very worrying time for him, and such was his pressing need for information from the hospital that he could not vacate the 'phone box until the race - the second on the card - was off.

With the 'phone line constantly giving the engaged signal, Yellow Sam's odds remained static: in the on-course market he was friendless, and as the runners came under orders he was still the 20-1 outsider. As soon as the field had set off, with Satlan and Philipine Hill disputing the lead, that price of 20-1 became the returned SP, and then all hell broke loose as those in the know on the course rushed in to back Yellow Sam in running. The 20-1 disappeared in an instant, and as the runners made their way around the tight Bellewstown track a frenzy of punting saw him backed at all prices down to 2-1, with some bookmakers wiping his name off their boards as soon as they realised what was afoot. Meanwhile the stout man had given up trying to find news of his sick relative and vacated the 'phone booth.

The most meticulously plotted coup can falter through equine frailty, but not this one. Yellow Sam moved up to dispute the lead at the third of the thirteen flights of hurdles, took it up before the fourth, and was never headed thereafter. Pushed into a decent lead before the last flight, he ran on to win by two and a half lengths from Glenallen.

One figure who had not been seen scampering around the ring taking prices in running was Curley himself. He was not even on the course to watch the fun, but casually walked through the entrance after the race was over, nonchalantly enquiring of the man at the turnstile: "What won the second?"

The exact amount which the plotters of the coup netted is not known, but Barney Curley does not dispute the usual estimate of around £300,000. His own share of the proceeds went towards the purchase of a 30-room Georgian mansion in County Westmeath, Middleton Park, which brought him widespread fame when he raffled the house and found himself sentenced to three months in prison for contravening the Gaming and Lotteries Act. The sentence was reduced on appeal to one of probation, one condition being that Curley donate £5,000 to the local branch of the St. Vincent de Paul Society - which amount he quickly doubled.

Having broken his duck, Yellow Sam himself returned to the winner's enclosure after his next race, a handicap hurdle at Wexford. On this occasion his price was a mere 5-2. He was sent to the Doncaster Autumn Sales and bought for 4,900 guineas to go to trainer Ken Oliver, but did not win again.

The Gay Future coup less than a year before had skirted the edge of illegality and just slipped over. Following a prosecution brought by the police, Tony Murphy, the brains behind the scheme, and trainer Anthony Collins, the Scottish based permit holder, were later convicted of conspiracy to defraud bookmakers. But there was no moral problem in the case of Yellow Sam. Not for the first time, the bookies had been had, and they knew it, though the coup hastened moves to bring in more secure blower systems to the on-course representatives of off-course layers. And henceforth any runner connected with Barney Curley would be watched with sometimes disproportionate interest.

The starting price coup which hinged on an occupied telephone box went straight into Irish racing lore. But whether the stout man's relative repaid his touching concern by making a full recovery has not been recorded.

*   *   *

Conclusion by R.O.: Despite frequent, and vigorously expressed, misgivings about the opportunities for punting afforded by the bookmaking industry, Barney Curley has survived privation stoically, while, nevertheless, contriving to strike some unexpected blows at the ring, since transferring his operation to England.

On 17th July 1991 the apprentice Tony D'Arcy, who claimed the 7 lbs. allowance, appeared in the racecard, published in the morning papers, as the rider of his five-year old Threshfield in the Harpers & Queen Handicap at the Sandown Park evening meeting. In the event the name of classic winning jockey John Reid appeared in the number board, and after being backed from 6/1 to clear favouritism at 3/1. Threshfield ran on strongly under 9st. 7 lbs. to win by two lengths. Mr. Curley was estimated to have won £90,000 over the race.

"Kenneth Baker (the then Home Secretary) says we've got to help ourselves, - well, I have", said the Master Punter, on being asked to comment on the outcome and the change of rider.

Three weeks later Threshfield was declared for the Jim Gundill Memorial Handicap at Pontefract, without any jockey in the morning papers. To the delight of the Pontefract racegoers, Lester Piggott unexpectedly arrived to take his only ride of the day on Mr. Curley's horse. Starting hot favourite at 11/10, Threshfield responded to powerful assistance from the saddle by holding on by a head. Happily, therefore, Mr. Curley has not been as badly starved of opportunities to ply his trade, as his eloquent complaints about the layers might lead us to suppose.

*   *   *

Sean Magee was born of Irish descent at Hampstead in 1949, and was named after the jockey who rode Solford to win the Champion Hurdle in 1940.

He is an expert on racing in both England and Ireland. His book *Racing and The Irish* (Stanley Paul, 1992) was widely acclaimed.

After reading English at St John's College, Cambridge, Sean Magee spent seventeen years in academic publishing until he wrote *The Channel Four Book of Racing* in 1979. He is also the Editor of *The Channel Four Book of The Racing Year,* as well as *Oaksey on Racing, The Daily Telegraph Flat Racing Year Book* and *The Racehorse Owners' Magazine.*

THE FAIRY TALE FLUTTER

(Aldaniti's 1981 Grand National)

Introduction by R.O.: For more than a century and a half, since it was first won by the appropriately named Lottery in 1839, the Grand National has been more deeply steeped in drama than any other race on earth. The roll of honour includes such great horses as Cloister, Manifesto and Aintree specialist Red Rum, while in contrast to those giants, winners include such unlikely animals as Chandler, bought from beneath the shafts of a gig at a meet of foxhounds in 1848; the crooked-legged Salamander, who had come from a job lot, in 1866; Casse Tete, the little chestnut mare bought out of a seller, in 1872; Tipperary Tim, the tubed, one-eyed outsider, who was the only horse to complete the course without mishap in 1928, and Foinavon, who was so far behind that he was able to avoid the fiasco at the twenty third fence by jumping on the wide outside.

Many a light of other days, or other apparently forlorn prospects, contest the race while owners hope against hope that some miracle will bring them steeplechasing immortality by making them Grand National winners too. Sometimes there are as many dreams as fences.

Just occasionally the whole nation shares a dream. It happened in 1981, when Bob Champion rode Aldaniti, owned by Mr. Nick Embericos and trained by former champion jockey Josh Gifford. Everybody wanted them to win. Only his enormous courage, and inflexible determination to ride Aldaniti at Aintree, had enabled Bob Champion to endure the six excruciating courses of chemotherapy that had effected the cure of his cancer, while Josh Gifford, most loyal of men, assured him that the job as stable jockey was waiting for him. Bob returned to the saddle on Roadhead at Stratford-on-Avon on 30th August 1980, and three weeks later rode his first winner for almost eighteen months on Physicist at Fontwell.

Even while Bob Champion was on the way back to to the top of his profession, Aldaniti seemed a singularly unlikely Grand National winner. Shortly after winning over hurdles at Ascot as a five-year-old in January 1975, Aldaniti had broken down on his off fore. Thereafter he was beset by leg trouble. He had been pulled up lame at Sandown Park in November on his only appearance of the season of 1979/80, and was off the course for fourteen months until Bob Champion rode him to win the Whitbread Trial Handicap Chase at Ascot as an 11-year-old on 11th February 1991, just seven weeks before his momentous triumph in the Grand National.

* * *

Graham Sharpe tells of one of those rare occasions when the bookmakers were actually happy to pay out over a big race winner which had been heavily backed by the public. As Lord Macaulay wrote in the his epic poem of of *How Horatius Held The Bridge,* "Even the ranks of Tuscany could scarce forbear to cheer" when Bob Champion won the Grand National on Aldaniti in1981.

* * *

It was a headline writer's dream - the true life story which no scriptwriter would ever dare concoct for fear of being accused of mawkish sentimentality. It was the bet which just HAD to win - which of the fates would have dared to conspire to prevent it from happening?

Everyone seemed to know what was going to happen - it was one of those very rare occasions - not unique, but definitely infrequent - when a feeling of inevitability sweeps over even the most hardened of bookmakers.

They just know that a certain horse is going to win a certain race and that they are powerless to do anything but sit back and savour the inevitability and join in the congratulations and celebrations when it happens. But, in a bizarre way, they really don't mind, probably because it doesn't happen that often!

It happened when Princess Anne married Captain Mark Phillips and Royal Mark won the Royal Wedding Chase at 11/10.

It happened when Red Rum won the National for the third time and when Desert Orchid won the Gold Cup for the first.

It happened in 1992 when, just days before a General Election, Party Politics won the National.

And, on the most emotional occasion of all, it happened in the 1981 Grand National when "two old crocks" (the jockey's words), Aldaniti, and rider Bob Champion, triumphed in the world's greatest race.

But what turned out to be one of the hugest public gambles ever to take place started somewhat inauspiciously when the horse's trainer, Josh Gifford, deliberately halved the bet the owner wanted to stake. Nick Embiricos, away on a ski-ing holiday, had rung Gifford to ask him to put £500 each way on Aldaniti at the prevailing National odds of 66/1. "Don't be silly", Gifford allegedly replied, "its 66/1 that he'll even get there, let alone win!" Surely the pair's relationship could not have survived after a stroke like that had cost the owner extra winnings of some twenty grand!

Not only did it survive - in fact, it flourished, and shipbroker Mr. Embiricos told me, "The story of my bet through Josh Gifford is absolutely correct - of course I forgave him for not putting on the whole lot! Shortly after collecting my winnings I received a letter from the bookmaker concerned, inviting me to bet with them more often!" There you are, I told you even the bookies knew the horse would win and accepted it with good grace.

Mr. Embiricos also added, "There must have been a huge amount of emotional money put on the horse on the day."

Indeed, there was, as Bob Champion was able to confirm to me, "I'd never had the sort of response that occurred after winning the National on Aldaniti. I had thousands of letters, many of them telling me that people had had bets on us because of my illness and because of Aldaniti's comeback from injury."

This partnership of a patched up horse and a written off jockey who had taken on and fought off the dread disease, cancer, combined to produce one of the heftiest public plunges of all, which cost Britain's bookies scores of millions but which they paid almost happily, brushing away the odd tear of joy in the process - partially placated by the fact that it had happened in the National when there were one or two losing bets left in their satchels, too!

The Embiricos long-range speculation, placed the Christmas before the race, was probably the greatest single wager placed on the outcome of the race, but there was no shortage of lesser bets, all equally important to those who had placed them, even if they were only seeking confirmation that out there in the chaos there is some kind of order which demands that bravery in adversity ultimately receives its due reward.

One of the letters Bob received was from Geoff Moorhouse, the father of a young patient who had recovered from the same type of cancer. "We always look out for your mounts to see how you are faring and we have even had a bet or two on you." Bob's nurse Carol, who helped him win his fight against cancer risked £3 on him in the big race - not a bad bet on a nurse's salary. Even before the race an old age pensioner wrote; "My prayers, your hopes and my wager will be on you on Saturday."

Another nurse who had worked in the hospital where Bob was treated wrote, "I remember you stopping me excitedly just outside the out-patients department where you told me the doctors had given you the fantastic news that your treatment had been a success and you were all clear. I can still remember your face as I had never seen you smile before in several months. I wish you luck in the Grand National and I shall have a few bob riding on you."

Two members of a profession popularly believed to be even harder of heart than bookmakers, were moved to thank Bob. They were Bank managers from Wootton Bassett, one of whom explained, "Might I explain that several members of my staff here are richer than they were on Friday night?"

The other said only, "Let me know in advance if you are going to do it again." Of course it couldn't happen again - and even though the pair made it back to the starting line again for the 1982 National it was all somewhat anti-climactic and they fell at the first fence.

But twelve months earlier Bob had been confident that nothing could go wrong, either for himself or for the millions whose bets were riding on him: "I knew I was the one people were backing - and I genuinely never thought we could be beaten. I'd been saying for years that Aldaniti was a National horse and the only danger was the first fence. After that I never felt a moment's worry."

Sixteen and a half million people watching the National on British TV had wagered an estimated £30,000,000 on the outcome of the race which was also being watched in seventeen other countries. Aldaniti and Bob Champion went off at 10/1, but bearing in mind that this was only Aldaniti's second racecourse appearance in sixteen months, having been plagued with injury throughout his career, perhaps the bookmakers were being less than generous despite those misgivings that only another 'Foinavon' foul-up could prevent the pair coming out on top.

The race was sponsored by *The Sun* newspaper, and the fact that it offered the biggest jumping prize money ever of £51,324 to the winner is probably part of the reason why the Embiricos-Gifford relationship remained firm despite half of that mega-bet having been surrendered.

Many people also tend to forget that the horse who finished second in the National in 1981 and actually started 8/1 favourite, provided almost as good a human interest story as the winner, and those shrewd punters who believed that a fairy tale deserved a suitable conclusion cashed in by backing the pair to finish winner and runner up in a forecast.

Spartan Missile who was bred, owned, trained and ridden by fifty four year old grandfather John Thorne finished just four lengths behind Aldaniti at the line - not that Champion was ever aware of the threat posed; "I always thought that Spartan Missile had fallen early on" he revealed.

At the time the future of the Grand National was in some doubt, and the 1981 result moved the prestigious *Chasers & Hurdlers Annual* to declare, "If we had to write a scenario for the 1981 Grand National with the object of convincing the doubters that the National is worth saving we could not have improved on the real thing."

The sponsors of the race, *The Sun,* certainly agreed with that assessment. Their front page story about the race on Monday, April 6, 1981, was headlined "Courage Of A Champion". "The nation cheered as Bob, 32, rode Aldaniti to glory - But the cheers were not just for his victory in the world's toughest horse race. They were for the bravery of a man who in June 1979 was told - 'You have only eight months to live'." Grand National historian Reg Green whose book *A Race Apart* describes every National which has taken place declared that it was "The finest result possible. Through the freely-flowing tears everybody smiled."

He was right, it was the day everyone smiled - particularly the millions of winning punters and even the losing bookies!

*   *   *

179

Conclusion by R.O.: In the euphoria that surrounded the magnificent success of Bob Champion on Aldaniti, many people lost sight of the superb professional skill of Josh Gifford, who was responsible for an eleven-year-old, with a long history of unsoundness, winning the Grand National. With characteristic modesty, Josh Gifford always maintains that Aldaniti would never have won the Aintree marathon, had he not been a very clean winded horse, who did not need a great deal of strong work, which would have imposed heavy demands on his legs, in order to bring him to peak form.

Josh Gifford never won the Grand National as a jockey, but given even a modicum of his share of luck, he would have done so on Honey End, when only Foinavon negotiated the twenty third fence at the first attempt in 1967. Trained by the late Captain Ryan Price at Findon, Honey End was backed from 100/8 to clear favourite at 15/2, but was amongst those hopelessly baulked as the riderless Popham Down ran across the twenty third. Presented at the fence for a second time, Honey End jumped like a stag, but by that time, Foinavon was a distance ahead of those runners that had got back into the race. All the same, Honey End made up ground to such good effect that he was only beaten fifteen lengths.

*   *   *

Graham Sharpe is Media Relations Manager of the William Hill Organisation. He was born in 1950, and lives in Middlesex. Having commenced his career with the *Weekly Post* Group in 1968, he is the author of various books on racing and gambling, including *Ready Reckoner* (in collaboration with M. J. Raper, Pan 1984), *Rare Stakes* (Pan, 1986), and *The Book of Amazing Bets* (Sporting Life, 1988). In addition he is a a regular contributor to *Betting Office Supplies Magazine* (B.O.S.), edited by Peter Fiddes.

In 1982, Graham Sharpe was nominated Argos Consumer Journalist of The Year.

WILLIAM PEARCE'S LAST WINNER

(Father Hayes' Win at Sandown in 1992)

Introduction by R.O.: Rumours were rife after Father Hayes had gone South from Yorkshire to bring off a massive gamble at Sandown Park in the middle of June 1992. His form was a long way from being inspiring, and speculation as to his being a ringer was fuelled by the knowledge that he had been previously registered as Highland Johnny and Dashing John, and there appeared to be irregularities in his documentation.

Father Hayes was trained by forty two year old Will Pearce, who had studied economics and finance at Surrey University, but only obtained a third class degree, as his heart was in racing. At the age of twenty one, he began a period of two years as pupil assistant to Colin Davies at St. Arvans near Chepstow. Subsequently he was assistant to the late Richmond Sturdy and Mick Gosden, for whom he rode his first winner. In the summer of 1989 he purchased the historic Hambleton House stable for almost £2.25 million. The following season he commenced training, and obtained his first success with Sharlie's Wimpy at Ripon in June 1984.

* * *

Grenville Davies gives an account of the extraordinary and controversial background of the American-bred Father Hayes, and the circumstances in which he brought off a sensational coup at Sandown Park.

* * *

As the amount and quality of racing information supplied to punters has improved over the years, particularly during the last decade, it has become increasingly more difficult for connections to land a gamble.

181

But now and then one crops up, and when it does, the minds of the racing public tend to be entranced, as if they are looking for some sort of skullduggery, only to find out, more often than not, that nothing of the sort has taken place.

So the victory of Father Hayes in the Hanover Square Handicap at Sandown on Saturday 13th June 1992, proved to be no exception. However this one had a decidedly tragic twist in the tail.

The horse had no worthwhile form to its name, added to which was the fact that he was lacking in experience, having had just four previous outings, all in the space of seven weeks.

His racecourse debut was in Hereford's Grunwick National Hunt Flat Race over one mile and five furlongs. He must have been showing a fair degree of ability at home, for having opened at 8-1, he was eventually returned at 'carpet' (3-1) only to finish sixth. No matter what performance he put up, it's very unlikely that much media attention would have been given to him for it just happened to be Grand National day.

Just nine days later on April 13th he took part in Edinburgh's mile and a half Inveresk Maiden Stakes. Starting at 20-1, he finished sixth of nine.

After his first two races in quick succession, it was another five weeks before he set foot on a racecourse again. In what proved to be a definite improvement in form, he ran in the one mile 100 yards Windmill Inn Maiden Stakes at Beverley on May 19th. Being slowly away over a distance too short for him, he made late progress to finish fourth.

Four days later he ran at Southwell on the All-Weather in the one mile Randall Maiden Stakes, but finished well down the field.

Every dog, or in this case, horse has his day and Father Hayes' was just around the corner. Sandown is about 250 miles from the historic training centre of Hambleton in North Yorkshire. Hambleton House has seen many a great trainer send out horses from its stables, the most famous being Noel Murless, (later Sir), who trained there in the mid 1940's. Its incumbent from 1989 until 1992 was William Pearce.

Substantial backing on the morning of the race saw the horse's price contract from 20-1 to 3's, by which time the bookmakers felt that something big was under way, particularly from a stable which was not known for throwing its money about. As that day's racing was being televised on Channel 4, John McCririck went on air, to let the public at home know of the catch that was about to be landed.

Once the on-course market opened it was an entirely different kettle of fish. Having opened at 7-2 Father Hayes was allowed to drift out to 11-2, before finally settling at 4-1 joint favourite. It would, however, be reasonable to assume that the majority of the money bet on course was from off-course outlets trying to reduce their liabilities, as well as racegoers joining in, because after all they are only human and hate the feeling of being left out, especially where money is concerned. One thing worth remembering is that the market at Sandown is a strong one, and it would have taken a welter of money to force a horse's price down from 11-2 to 4-1.

Carrying 9 st. 9lb. in a 0-70 Handicap he was drawn 9 of 12 and ridden by David Nicholls. Having tracked the leaders for most of the race, Father Hayes took up the running three furlongs out and ran out an easy two and a half length winner from Smiling Chief. As they passed the winning post, David Nicholls jubilantly punched the air, in a style reminiscent of Jonjo O'Neill. This if nothing else was a family success for the horse was owned by Will Pearce's brother Rodney, although he claimed not to have had much on.

At the subsequent post race interviews the trainer talked about the coup in a very open manner: "I don't bet heavily apart from the occasional two-year-old, but a lot of my owners do. This time was an exception but I don't want you thinking that I can buy Blenheim Palace. An unraced four-year-old is an unusual thing. He came to us from a livery yard. I believe there had been problems over documentation or problems after he came over from the States. I had to get him qualified for handicaps and after the Southwell race, when he hated the track, the extra distance plus the mark he had been given made us fancy him a bit".

The racecourse stewards took the decision to question both trainer and jockey about the horse's apparent improvement in form, compared to his previous races. The explanations given were that he had run green at Edinburgh, while at Southwell and Beverley he had been unsuited by the shorter trips. The handicapper also said that Father

Hayes had probably not been suited by the Southwell surface. The explanations were accepted.

It was only then that rumours started to spread, claiming the horse was not the one he was supposed to be, a ringer in other words. Especially when it became apparent that the horse had been registered previously under two different names, although he did not run under either.

It was at this juncture that the Jockey Club decided to delve further. So three days after the race on 16th June a statement was issued from Portman Square saying: "The Jockey Club is taking steps to establish that the correct horse was running in the name of Father Hayes. The Security Department are also looking into other aspects of the affair."

Only the previous day the horse's trainer William Pearce had been found shot dead at his stables, all the makings of a good Dick Francis novel. However, in this case, fact was indeed stranger than fiction.

What came to light was that as a yearling Father Hayes was sold at Keeneland's September Sales. Bloodstock agent Charles Gordon-Watson was listed as the buyer. However, since then he has denied any involvement whatsoever with the chestnut son of Stage Door Johnny and Fleur D'or. This incidentally made him a half brother to a decent juvenile hurdler in Highland Bud, who finished second in the 1989 Daily Express Triumph Hurdle, when owned by Sheikh Mohammed and trained by David Nicholson.

Now the horse's problems or rather his owner's were only just beginning, for on October 17th 1989 the American Jockey Club allowed the then un-named yearling to go to Ireland, but Weatherby's said "where he went to is anybody's guess". There is no record of the horse leaving Ireland for Britain, the reason being that none is required by mutual agreement between the two countries.

The horse was initially named Highland Johnny when he appeared in *Horses in Training 1990*, his trainer being Dermot Browne, who was later warned off for ten years for selling information to a bookmaker.

In that particular edition of *Horses in Training* Highland Johnny's colour was given as bay. More than likely this was not an attempt to hoodwink people, but rather human error, for Len Bell, the book's editor, said at the time: "When two-year-olds are included, all the details are provided by the stable concerned and mistakes can occur.

184

We have no way of double checking the details until they get older".
This view was also substantiated by a Jockey Club Official.

His owner then was Irish Publican, Tony Gleeson, who was not
adverse to a tilt at the ring himself, having won more than a few bob
when his own horse Rotherfield Greys won the 1988 Stewards Cup.

Gleeson attempted to sell the horse to David Nicholson. However,
the Duke had second thoughts and backed out over the lack of
registration papers. This no doubt caused Gleeson to come to an
agreement with Keeneland about the money still owed from the
original sale.

One thing definite about the horse's past is the fact that he had
arrived in England by November 25th 1991, and was registered at
Weatherby's as Dashing John.

Four months later he became Father Hayes. Not many four-year-
olds could claim to having such an eventful life and yet not have been
near a racecourse.

After viewing the film of the Hanover Square Handicap, the Jockey
Club came to the conclusion that the horse who won the said race had
markings consistent with those registered for Father Hayes.

So far I've neglected to mention the amount of money won off the
bookmakers both on and off the course. The exact figure will never be
known, but various figures have been bandied about from as little as
£50,000 to as much as £500,000. Also you have to remember that the
amount won by the horse's connections obviously differs from how
much was actually won.

On 24th June 1992 The Jockey Club issued a press release saying:
"The Jockey Club has completed analysis of blood samples taken from
Father Hayes (USA), a four-year-old chestnut gelding, by Stage Door
Johnny (USA) out of Fleur D'Or (USA).

Two samples have been analysed, the first having been obtained
during routine sampling after the horse's success on Saturday 13th
June, and the second having been taken at the training yard early the
following week. The samples have been shown to be of an identical
blood type, and the American Jockey Club has confirmed that on the
evidence of this blood type there is no basis for exclusion of the horse
from the parentage registered in the American Stud Book.

Taken in conjunction with the satisfactory check already carried out on the horse's markings, the Jockey Club is entirely satisfied that the horse which ran in the Hanover Square Handicap at Sandown was Father Hayes (USA).

This has concluded the Jockey Club's consideration of the running of this horse".

After the death of Will Pearce, his head lad, Ben Beasley took over the licence. Father Hayes' next outing was at Newcastle on the Friday evening of June 26th in the Dataform Handicap, over one mile four furlongs, where he finished well down the field, so fuelling the arguments of the believers that something untoward had gone off. After that he did not run again during the 1992 flat season due to a blood infection.

*　　*　　*

Conclusion by R .0.: The successful coup brought off with Father Hayes was to have an immediate aftermath of stark tragedy. Just two days later, shortly after noon on Monday 15th June, the body of Will Pearce, with a 12-bore shotgun on the grass beside him, was found in a small wood close to the gallops.

The Thirsk coroner, Jeremy Cave, recorded a verdict of suicide, without being able to elicit a motive. Whatever reason Will Pearce may have had for taking his own life, it can have had nothing to do with Father Hayes winning at Sandown Park. As Grenville Davies has shown, the horse brought off a cleverly planned gamble, without there having been any recourse to breaking the rules, contrary to the import of all the rumour and gossip, which was so greatly intensified by the death of the trainer.

*　　*　　*

Grenville Davies has been interested in racing since he backed Tied Cottage for the 1979 Gold Cup, and saw him fall while disputing the lead at the last fence. He is a regular contributor to *Racing Advisor,* formerly *Come Racing,* and wrote a brief history of Nottingham Racecourse, which was included in the Colwick Park racecards in 1992, the course's centenary year. The Secretary of the East Midlands Racing Club, he has contributed to research for a book on extinct

186

courses, and is currently writing *"A Touch of Colwick - The History of Nottingham Racecourse"*. He works for Nottinghamshire County Council as a library assistant.

188

RUNNERS INCLUDED IN VOLUME 1

PRINCE OF WALES' JOCKEY WARNED OFF
(The Escape Affair of 1791)

THE PLOT AGAINST JERRY
(The 1824 St Leger)

LORD GEORGE V. LEVI GOODMAN
(The Ringers in 1844 Epsom Derby)

A TRIPLE DEAD HEAT
(Prioress' 1857 Cesarewitch Victory)

THE LONDONERS' SALOON BAR CHAMPION
(Victor Wild's 1895 Great Jubilee Win)

THE FOILING OF A FRENCH GAMBLE
(Epinard and the Cambridgeshire of 1923)

£100,000,000 FAILURE
(Tudor Minstrel and the 1947 Derby)

THE GAMBLE THAT MADE A CAREER
(Barry Hills & Frankincense's 1968 Lincoln Win)

A NORTHERN RINGER IN 1982
(The Flockton Grey Story)

THE MODERN IRISH MIDAS
(Noel Furlong and the 1991 National Hunt Festival)

RUNNERS INCLUDED IN VOLUME 2

A NOBBLER HANGED IN 1812
(Dan Dawson, The Poisoner)

THE FINAL ROTHSCHILD COUP OF 1871
(The Cesarewitch Gamble on Corisande)

**SIR GEORGE CHETWYND VERSUS THE EARL
OF DURHAM**
(The Most Famous Court Case in 1889)

THE RACE MEETING THAT NEVER WAS
(The Trodmore Hunt in 1898)

THE VERY FURTIVE TRIAL OF ST. LOUIS
(Peter Purcell Gilpin and The 2,000 Guineas of 1922)

LADIES POINT-TO-POINTER LANDS ENORMOUS BETS
(Fly Away II's Win at The 1948 Southdown Point-to-Point)

AN EXPENSIVE NECK IN THE GRAND NATIONAL
(Alec Bird and Tudor Line In 1954)

HOW ALCIDE WAS 'GOT AT'
(The Captain Denied Another Derby in 1958)

ARKLE RESCUES A BOOKIE
(Arkle's First Win at Navan in 1962)

SIR IVOR WINS THE DERBY AT 100 TO 1
(Raymond Guest's Bet with William Hill on The 1968 Derby)